Business Interactions

Candace Matthews

Kuwait University

Drawings by
Paul Stephen Docksey

PRENTICE HALL REGENTS
Upper Saddle River, NJ 07458

Library of Congress Cataloging-in-Publication Data

Matthews, Candace (date)
  Business interactions.

  1. English language—Business English. 2. English
language—Text-books for foreign speakers.
3. Communication in management. I. Title.
PE1115.M37 1987   428.3′4′02465   86–30373
ISBN 0–13–100876–5

The photographs in the text are reprinted by courtesy of the following sources:

Page 5, clockwise from upper left: © Michal Heron 1982; A.T.&T. Co. Photo Center; © Michal Heron 1982; A.T.&T. Co. Photo Center; Minnesota Tourism Division; Irene Springer. *Page 55, clockwise from upper left:* Laimute E. Druskis (two photos); Redwood Empire Association; Prentice-Hall Photo Archives; Irene Springer. *Page 56, top to bottom:* Larry Fleming; Canadian Pacific; Eleanor D'Antuono/American Ballet Theatre. *Page 144:* Underwood Company (top left); International Business Machines Corporation.

Cover design: Lundgren Graphics, Ltd.
Manufacturing buyer: Carol Bystrom

©1987 by Prentice Hall Regents
Prentice-Hall, Inc.
A Simon & Schuster Company
Upper Saddle River, NJ 07458

Printed in the United States of America

20 19 18 17 16 15 14 13 12 11

ISBN   0-13-100876-5

Prentice-Hall International (UK) Limited, *London*
Prentice-Hall of Australia Pty. Limited, *Sydney*
Prentice-Hall Canada Inc., *Toronto*
Prentice-Hall Hispanoamericana, S.A., *Mexico*
Prentice-Hall of India Private Limited, *New Delhi*
Prentice-Hall of Japan, Inc., *Tokyo*
Prentice-Hall of Southeast Asia Pte. Ltd., *Singapore*
Editora Prentice-Hall do Brasil, Ltda., *Rio de Janeiro*

Contents

Unit 9   *158*

Unit 10   *177*

Appendices   *201*

Contents Overview

	Functions	*Discussion Techniques*	*Communication Concepts*
Unit 6	Getting further information Asking for clarification Clarifying your own ideas Paraphrasing another person's ideas	Avoiding answering	Effective listening
Unit 7	Supporting an idea or suggestion Opposing an idea or suggestion Asking for examples Giving examples	Correcting yourself	Group task roles
Unit 8	Asking about preferences Comparing Showing similarities	Keeping the discussion moving	Group building roles
Unit 9	Asking about alternatives Asking about consequences Predicting consequences Expressing possibility	Returning to the subject	Individual blocking roles
Unit 10	Persuading and convincing Counterarguing Conceding	Summarizing	Nonverbal communication

Preface

Purpose

The purpose of *Business Interactions* is to develop the oral communication skills of EFL/ESL students of business. Functional in approach, the text focuses on teaching students the skills they need in order to interact effectively in small group discussions. The material is organized to help the students:

- become familiar with common business concepts, terms, and expressions
- understand the basic principles of group interaction
- build up the speaking skills necessary for appropriate communication in English
- learn how to participate effectively in problem solving discussions based on business situations
- comprehend the major points of group discussions
- evaluate the effectiveness of their own and others' small group discussions

Types of Students

This book is intended for:

- business people at an intermediate to advanced level of English who want to practice speaking English in a business context
- business studies students and management trainees who need to improve their command of spoken English

Components

The complete course consists of:

- This book
- Instructor's Manual
- Cassette

Acknowledgments

In writing this book I discovered how many people it actually takes to write a book attributed to one author. I would like to thank all of the people who contributed to this book in so many ways.

In particular, I would like to thank the following people for their special efforts: Kathleen Burke, Joanne Marino, and Will Gagner, for piloting much of the material and providing useful feedback; Musa'ab Meinke, for reviewing the original manuscript and offering many helpful suggestions; Ernie Matthews, Debbie Bonte, and Pam Mangan, for their assistance with the original manuscript; Victor Mason, for his thorough review of the Instructor's Manual; Ralph Hosmer, for his useful comments on the Instructor's Manual; Tina Carver and Brenda White of Prentice-Hall, for their help with all aspects of the project; and Doug Gordon, for his valuable advice in the production of the book.

I would like to express my gratitude to Dr. Balkees Al Najjar, head of the Language Centre of Kuwait University, for her cooperation in the making of the listening tape. I am especially grateful to Mohammed Mo'awwad for his technical expertise as well as the time and effort he put into producing the tape. My sincere thanks go to my friends and colleagues who helped in the recording of the tape: Liz Nakhoul, Ralph Hosmer, Marianne Hill, Sara Mabie, Karen Gwaltney-Beaumont, David Tyler, Harold (Skip) Wilcox, Nigel Bruce, Michael Plumb, Paul Seng, Jane Gaffney, Doug Thomas, and Philip Erith.

I would like to express my appreciation to two friends for their unfailing support and encouragement over the years: Michael Barrett and Don Henderson. Finally, I would like to thank Alan Lennox for his support in this and every project.

I dedicate this book to my mother and father.

Introduction:
To the Student

This book will give you practice in speaking English in business situations. As you go through the exercises, you will learn how to express your ideas more clearly in English. You will also become familiar with common business terms and expressions. This book will help you improve your speaking skills so that you are able to participate effectively in small group discussions.

Each unit generally consists of the following sections:

Phrases	This section contains lists of some phrases that are used to express different functions in English. Since not all possible phrases are included, class members may want to suggest additional phrases for each function.
Listening Practice	These exercises give you practice in comprehending spoken English. They also help you become familiar with the way the phrases are used by English speakers.
Controlled Practice	This section contains exercises to give you practice in using the phrases. You may not go over all of the examples in the exercises, but the instructor will give you enough practice so that you can remember the phrases and use them correctly.

The purpose here is for you to try to use as many different phrases as possible so that you can add variety to your language. The more phrases you are able to use, the more effective you can be as a speaker. Also, these exercises give you a chance to work on correcting your grammar mistakes, adding to your vocabulary, and improving your pronunciation.

Communication Concepts

This section gives you information on how good business meetings should be carried out in English. It also explains some of the basic principles of group interaction.

Discussion Techniques

This section includes brief explanations of some of the special techniques used in a small group discussion.

Role Playing

This section contains four role plays based on different business situations. The instructor or class members can choose the role plays that are the most interesting to the students in your class. This means that your class may not do all of the role plays in each unit—just the ones that are the most useful to your particular group. It is also possible for two or three groups to perform the same role play. One group can start where the other group finishes, or the groups can try to discuss different solutions to the problem.

Four or five students should perform a role play with the rest of the class acting as observers. If there are only three roles in a role play, two students can take the same role. Students performing the role play should look at each other, not at the observers or the instructor.

Each discussion should last from ten to fifteen minutes. Since this is usually not enough time for a group to reach a final decision, the focus is on group members *interacting* while working toward a solution to the problem.

The first two units show you how to prepare for the role play. You can follow the same steps in getting ready for role plays in later units. This preparation is important since it helps you develop good ideas that you can use in the discussion.

It is important to have a class atmosphere in which everyone feels comfortable about speaking and participating in the discussions. You should not worry about making mistakes. Everybody makes mistakes. The key to success is to be able to learn from the mistakes you and the other students make.

An evaluation form is included after each role play to encourage you to pay careful attention to the other discussions. The questions in this form will also help you become aware of what makes a successful discussion.

Be sure to be open to both giving and receiving suggestions on how to improve the discussions. Learning to speak is not a competition. It is a group effort. You are all working toward the same goal—learning how to speak effectively in a group discussion. Some of your discussions, especially the early ones, will not be completely successful. But you, as well as the other students, can learn from your mistakes.

Useful Vocabulary

This is a list of useful vocabulary words that appear in each section. You can go over the meanings of the words for each section immediately before covering that section of the unit.

Unit 1

Phrases

This section contains lists of some phrases that are used to express different functions in English. Since not all possible phrases are included, you may want to add additional phrases for each function.

Giving an opinion
In my opinion, _____.
As far as I'm concerned, _____.
As I see it, _____.
Personally, I think _____.
It seems to me _____.
I think _____.
I believe _____.

Asking about agreement
Do you agree?
Don't you agree?
Wouldn't you agree?
Don't you think so?

Agreeing
Yes, that's true.   I agree with you.
That's right.   I definitely agree with you.
You're right.   I completely agree.
I think so, too.   That's a very good point.
That's a good idea.

Disagreeing
    I don't really agree with you.
    I don't think so.
    I'm afraid I can't agree with you.
    I'm not sure I quite agree with you.
    That's not how I see it.
    Yes, that may be true, but _____.
    Well, you have a point there, but _____.
    I can see your point, but _____.
    I see what you mean, but _____.

Listening Practice

Section 1. There are eight separate dialogs in this section. All of these dialogs are about the same general subject. A large retail department store has been losing sales for the past year.

A. Listen to the dialogs on the cassette. After you listen to each one, answer the question about what the first speaker in each dialog said. Circle the letter of the correct answer.

> *Example:* The woman thinks that the decline in sales _____ a serious problem.
>   a. is   b. is not

1. The man wants to _____ the store's image.
    a. keep   b. change

2. The woman prefers a _____ image for the store.
    a. traditional   b. modern

3. The man _____ the idea of self-service shopping in the store.
    a. doesn't like   b. likes

4. The woman wants to appeal to _____ customers.
    a. younger   b. older

5. The man wants to _____ the prices of the goods in the store.
    a. raise   b. lower

6. The woman wants to have _____ advertising.
    a. less   b. more

7. The man wants to _____ the number of employees.
    a. decrease   b. increase

8. The woman wants the store to offer _____ services.
    a. fewer   b. more

B. Now listen to the dialogs again. This time decide whether the second speaker agrees or disagrees with the first. Put a check [√] in the correct space.

	Agree	*Disagree*	*Phrase*
Example:	____	____	_____
1.	____	____	_____
2.	____	____	_____
3.	____	____	_____
4.	____	____	_____
5.	____	____	_____
6.	____	____	_____
7.	____	____	_____
8.	____	____	_____

C. Listen to the dialogs one more time. Write down the phrase in the list above that the second speaker uses to agree or disagree.

Section 2. There is one discussion in this section. It is about the following situation:

Some managers have just heard about a plan to introduce a system of merit pay bonuses for all of the managers in the company. Three managers are discussing this plan.

A. Listen to the discussion. How will the pay bonuses be determined?

_____

B. Look at the list of possible problems of merit pay bonuses. Which of these points do the speakers mention? Listen to the discussion again. Put a check [√] next to the ideas that are mentioned.

_____ 1. too much paperwork
_____ 2. productivity might be decreased
_____ 3. managers might compete too much
_____ 4. conflict between managers and superiors
_____ 5. bonuses aren't large enough
_____ 6. too much stress on managers

C. Listen again to the discussion. What phrases do the speakers use to introduce their opinions? Make a list of these phrases in the order that you hear them.

1. _____

2. _____

3. _____

4. _____

5. _____

6. _____

Controlled Practice

Exercise 1. Try to use some different phrases from the unit in discussing the illustrations on the following page.

  Speaker A: Give your opinion.

  Speaker B: Agree or disagree.

Exercise 2. Try to use some different phrases from the unit in discussing the following topics.

  Speaker A: Give an opinion on the topic. Then ask about agreement or disagreement.

  Speaker B: Agree or disagree.

1. the best _____
   a. airlines to fly
   b. restaurant in town
   c. hotel in the area
   d. city to live in
   e. foreign language to learn
   f. computer to buy
   g. country to visit for a vacation

2. the most _____
   a. useful office machine
   b. difficult business course
   c. relaxing holiday
   d. interesting sport
   e. important goal in life
   f. serious problem in the world
   g. important quality in a banker

What is the biggest $\begin{cases} \text{advantage?} \\ \text{disadvantage?} \end{cases}$

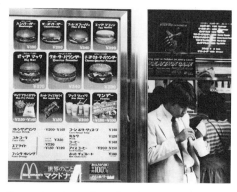

1. eating in a fast-food restaurant

2. sharing an office

3. being a manager

4. taking a bus to work

5. working in a factory

6. working with computers

3. the best way to _____
   a. find a job
   b. increase productivity in a factory
   c. invest your money
   d. advertise a new department store
   e. learn a language
   f. meet people
   g. spend your spare time

4. the biggest advantage [disadvantage] of _____
   a. working for a small company
   b. starting your own business
   c. owning a car
   d. having flexible working hours
   e. working the night shift
   f. living in a foreign country
   g. investing in the stock market

Exercise 3.   Try to use some different phrases from the unit in discussing the following topics.

> *Speaker A:*   Give an opinion on the topic. Then ask about agreement or disagreement.
>
> *Speaker B:*   Agree or disagree.

1. the best brand of watch to buy
2. the worst kind of boss to have
3. the most interesting program on television
4. the hardest part of a factory worker's job
5. the most important duty of a manager
6. the best way to entertain a client
7. the biggest advantage of having a university degree
8. the most economical car to buy
9. the most interesting job to have
10. the best way to reduce stress on the job
11. the fastest way to get to work
12. the easiest way to stop smoking
13. the best company in this country to work for
14. the worst part about going to meetings
15. the best way to cut costs
16. the most important job in a company
17. the best way to get out of doing work
18. the worst problem a working mother faces
19. the best way to get a promotion
20. the most useful skill in English (reading, speaking or writing)

Communication Concepts

Language Styles

Speakers of English can use different styles of language to communicate the same idea. For example, you may choose a formal or an informal style of saying the same thing:

Informal	Formal
Thanks.	Thank you very much.
Hi.	Good afternoon.
Sit down.	Would you care to sit down?
Can you give me a hand?	I'd certainly appreciate it if you could help me.
Great idea!	In my opinion, that is an excellent suggestion.

In most situations a neutral style of language (between formal and informal) is acceptable. However, a special situation may require you to use a more formal or informal style.

Discuss how each of the following factors might influence your choice of formal or informal English:

1. What is your relationship to the other speaker?
   a. relative
   b. friend
   c. acquaintance
   d. stranger

2. What is the other speaker's professional role?
   a. your colleague
   b. your superior
   c. your subordinate

3. What is the other speaker's age?
   a. much older than you
   b. much younger than you
   c. about the same age

4. What is the setting?
   a. a business meeting
   b. a job interview
   c. a formal dinner party
   d. a picnic

5. What subject are you discussing?
   a. everyday business matters
   b. a special favor that you want
   c. a serious complaint

Of course, most speaking situations involve some or all of these factors, not just one. Your choice of language style will depend on how these factors combine. For example, how do the following differences change the appropriate language style?

1. You are in a committee meeting
   { with only your colleagues.
    with a group of your superiors.

2. You are asking { your secretary / your boss } for help with a project.

3. You are talking with a friend
   { about a movie you saw last night.
    about lending you a large amount of money.

Fortunately, much of the language that you learn is neutral in style. Therefore, you can use it in both formal and informal situations. However, as you improve your speaking ability, you should also improve your ability to change your speaking style according to the subject, the situation, and the people involved.

Discussion Techniques

Introducing a Discussion

An introduction to a discussion should take only a minute or two and should cover the following points:

• *Greeting*
"Good { morning. / afternoon. / evening. } Thank you all for coming."

• *General statement of the subject*
"We're here today to talk about ＿＿＿＿＿＿＿."

• *Introduction of the participants*

"At our meeting today we have Mike Smith, who is a government official. Also, we have _____."

    or

"Why don't you introduce yourselves?"

• *Statement of the specific purpose or goal of the discussion*

"The $\left\{ \begin{array}{l} \text{purpose} \\ \text{goal} \end{array} \right\}$ of this discussion is to $\left\{ \begin{array}{l} \text{agree} \\ \text{decide} \\ \text{solve} \end{array} \right\}$ _____."

• *Opening the subject for discussion*

"Mary [or Ms. Jones], would you like to begin?"

    or

"Who would like to begin?"

Role Playing

This section contains four role plays. You and the instructor can choose the role plays that are the most interesting or the most useful to the students in your class. Four or five students can participate in each role play discussion. Students who observe the discussion can fill in the evaluation form following each role play.

Preparing for the Role Playing: Brainstorming

Before doing a role play it will help you to do some brainstorming. In a brainstorming session you get together with several other people to think of as many different ideas as possible to use in the discussion. Here are some points for group members to keep in mind during brainstorming:

- Feel free to suggest any idea that comes to mind.
- Do not stop to judge anyone's ideas.
- No idea is too stupid or too crazy.
- Try to improve or add to ideas suggested by others.
- The quantity of ideas is more important than the quality.
- Everyone should participate.
- All ideas should be written down without comment.

Once you have a long list of possible ideas, you can choose the best ones to use in the discussion. In the role plays in the first few units there are points to guide you during the brainstorming session. In later units you will be on your own to think of ideas.

Role Play 1A: Helping Retired Workers

Situation

Some retired workers have gone back to their old company to ask for help. They say that they feel useless now that they are no longer working. In addition, the retirees feel cut off from their friends, and face financial problems since their pensions have not kept up with inflation. Although the president of the company agrees that something should be done, there is not much money in the budget to spend. A meeting has been called to discuss this issue.

Purpose of the Discussion

The purpose of this discussion is for the group members to decide on the best ways that the company can help the retired workers.

Group Roles

Leader: the president of the company
Representative(s) of the retired workers
Company executive(s)

Brainstorming

What are some specific ways in which the company could improve the lives of the retired workers? Brainstorm as many ideas as possible. You can use the following list of general points to help you think of specific solutions:

- financial (more insurance? financial or legal counseling? additional pensions? special funds?)
- health (psychological counseling? dental or medical care? physical fitness classes?)

- social (organized activities? hobby center? special classes? travel?)
- food and housing (retirees eat in company cafeteria? food delivered to homes? help with house repairs?)
- work (part-time work in company? part-time work in other companies? volunteer work in community?)

Specific solutions:

1. _____
2. _____
3. _____
4. _____
5. _____
6. _____
7. _____
8. _____
9. _____
10. _____

Selecting Ideas

Consider the different ideas that you developed during the brainstorming session. Go back and select the best ideas for each role:

Retired Workers	*Company Executives*

Retired Workers | *Company Executives*

Starting the Discussion

Now you are ready to start the discussion. Your group should discuss the topic for ten minutes. Since this is not much time, do not worry if you do not reach a final decision. An important point to keep in mind is that *all* members should take part in the discussion.

Observing: Evaluating the Discussion

1. *Listening to the discussion*

   a. What is the purpose of this discussion? Be specific.

   _____

   _____

   b. As you listen to the discussion, make a list of the different solutions that the group members discuss.

   _____

   _____

   _____

   _____

   _____

2. *Follow-up to the discussion*

   Which of the solutions to the problem do *you* think is the best? Why?

   _____

   _____

3. *Rating the discussion*

Use the following scales to rate the discussion group:

Participation: Did all members take part equally?

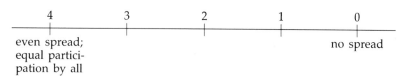

even spread;
equal partici-
pation by all

no spread

Pace: Did the discussion move along at the right speed?

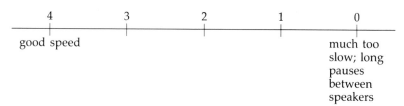

good speed

much too
slow; long
pauses
between
speakers

Role Play 1B: An Anti-Litter Campaign

Situation

The problem of litter has become quite serious in a large city. City officials want to have a clean city. They also want to stop people from littering. A meeting has been called to discuss this issue.

Purpose of the Discussion

The purpose of this discussion is for the group members to agree on the best ways to stop people from littering.

Group Roles

Leader: the head of the city government
Concerned resident(s)
City official(s)

Brainstorming

What are some specific ways to stop people from littering? Brainstorm as many ideas as possible. You can use the following list of general points to help you think of specific solutions:

- media (television? newspapers? radio? magazines?)
- education (schools? lectures? seminars?)
- business (advertising? recycling projects? litter containers? reminders on cups, bags, and wrappers?)
- service and social organizations (groups to clean up streets, parks, and other areas?)
- government (laws? penalties? rewards? clean-up week campaign?)

Specific solutions:

1. _____
2. _____
3. _____
4. _____
5. _____
6. _____
7. _____
8. _____
9. _____
10. _____

Selecting Ideas

Consider the different ideas that you developed during the brainstorming session. Go back and select the best ideas for each role:

Concerned Residents | *City Officials*

Concerned Residents   *City Officials*

Starting the Discussion

Now you are ready to start the discussion. Your group should discuss the topic for ten minutes. Since this is not much time, do not worry if you do not reach a final decision. An important point to keep in mind is that *all* members should take part in the discussion.

Observing: Evaluating the Discussion

1. *Listening to the discussion*

    a. What is the purpose of this discussion? Be specific.

    _____

    _____

    b. As you listen to the discussion, make a list of the different solutions that the group members discuss.

    _____

    _____

    _____

    _____

    _____

2. *Follow-up to the discussion*

Which of the solutions to the problem do *you* think is the best? Why?

_____

_____

3. *Rating the discussion*

Use the following scales to rate the discussion group:

Participation: Did all members take part equally?

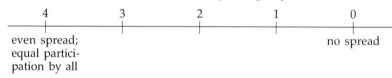

4   3   2   1   0

even spread; equal partici- pation by all   no spread

Pace: Did the discussion move along at the right speed?

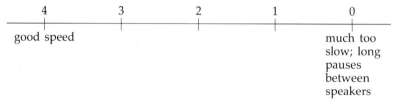

4   3   2   1   0

good speed   much too slow; long pauses between speakers

Role Play 1C: Solving the Traffic Problem

Situation

Government officials are worried about the rapid increase in the number of cars in the city. This large city has serious traffic problems that will soon be impossible to control. Therefore, city officials want to reduce the number of cars as soon as possible. A meeting has been called to discuss this issue.

Purpose of the Discussion

The purpose of this discussion is for the group members to agree on the best ways to reduce the number of cars in the city.

Group Roles

Leader: the head of the city government
City official(s)
Representative(s) of car owners

Brainstorming

What are some specific ways to reduce the number of cars in the city? Brainstorm as many ideas as possible. You can use the following list of general points to help you think of specific solutions:

- legal (restrict licenses? increase fines? restrict cars in certain areas? car inspection? restrict parking?)
- media (advertising campaign?)
- financial (road tax? car registration fees? parking charges? gas tax? car tax?)
- private companies (bus service for employees? transportation manager?)
- alternatives (ride sharing? public transportation?)

Specific solutions:

1. _____
2. _____
3. _____
4. _____
5. _____
6. _____
7. _____
8. _____
9. _____
10. _____

Selecting Ideas

Consider the different ideas that you developed during the brain-storming session. Go back and select the best ideas for each role:

City Officials	*Car Owners*

Starting the Discussion

Now you are ready to start the discussion. Your group should discuss the topic for ten minutes. Since this is not much time, do not worry if you do not reach a final decision. An important point to keep in mind is that *all* members should take part in the discussion.

Observing: Evaluating the Discussion

1. *Listening to the discussion*

a. What is the purpose of this discussion? Be specific.

_____

_____

b. As you listen to the discussion, make a list of the different solutions that the group members discuss.

_____

_____

_____

_____

_____

2. *Follow-up to the discussion*

Which of the solutions to the problem do *you* think is the best? Why?

_____

_____

3. *Rating the discussion*

Use the following scales to rate the discussion group:

Participation: Did all members take part equally?

4	3	2	1	0
even spread; equal participation by all				no spread

Pace: Did the discussion move along at the right speed?

4	3	2	1	0
good speed				much too slow; long pauses between speakers

Role Play 1D: Improving Factory Conditions

Situation

The owner of a small, nonunionized manufacturing company has noticed an increase in absenteeism and tardiness among workers in the factory. Furthermore, the workers have been complaining a lot lately, but there doesn't seem to be one specific cause of their dissatisfaction. At the same time, there has been a slight decrease in productivity as well as a decline in the quality of factory products. Unfortunately, there is not enough money in the budget for pay raises, but the owner would like to improve the current situation. The owner has called a meeting to discuss this issue.

Purpose of the Discussion

The purpose of this discussion is for the group members to agree on the best ways of improving the employees' working conditions in the factory.

Group Roles

Leader: the owner of the factory
Employee representative(s)
Company executive(s)

Brainstorming

What are some specific ways in which the employees' working conditions can be improved? Brainstorm as many ideas as possible. You can use the following list of general points to help you think of specific solutions:

- communication between workers and management (number of meetings? number and kind of memos? suggestion box?)
- working hours (number of hours? flexible hours?)
- breaks (number and length of breaks? facilities for breaks?)
- days off (length of vacation? number of paid holidays, sick days, and personal days?)
- education and training (in-service training? paid tuition? time off for classes? financial rewards?)
- working environment (music? lighting? noise?)

Specific solutions:

1. _____

2. _____

3. _____

4. _____

5. _____

6. _____

7. _____

8. _____

9. _____

10. _____

Selecting Ideas

Consider the different ideas that you developed during the brainstorming session. Go back and select the best ideas for each role:

Employees	*Company Executives*

Starting the Discussion

Now you are ready to start the discussion. Your group should discuss the topic for ten minutes. Since this is not much time, do not worry if you do not reach a final decision. An important point to keep in mind is that *all* members should take part in the discussion.

Observing: Evaluating the Discussion

1. *Listening to the discussion*

   a. What is the purpose of this discussion? Be specific.

   _____

   _____

   b. As you listen to the discussion, make a list of the different solutions that the group members discuss.

   _____

   _____

   _____

   _____

   _____

2. *Follow-up to the discussion*

   Which of the solutions to the problem do *you* think is the best? Why?

   _____

   _____

3. *Rating the discussion*

   Use the following scales to rate the discussion group:

   Participation: Did all members take part equally?

4	3	2	1	0

   even spread;   no spread
   equal partici-
   pation by all

   Pace: Did the discussion move along at the right speed?

4	3	2	1	0

   good speed   much too
   slow; long
   pauses
   between
   speakers

Participant Self-Evaluation

After you participate in a discussion, answer the following questions:

1. Do you think you spoke $\begin{cases} \text{about the right amount?} \\ \text{too much?} \\ \text{not enough?} \end{cases}$

2. Did you ask $\begin{cases} \text{some questions?} \\ \text{no questions?} \end{cases}$

3. Did you use $\begin{cases} \text{some phrases?} \\ \text{no phrases?} \end{cases}$

4. Did you have any problems during the discussion? Check any of the following that apply to you:

_____ a. I didn't understand the topic.

_____ b. I had problems with vocabulary. I didn't know the words in English to say what I wanted.

_____ c. I had problems with grammar.

_____ d. I haven't had enough practice in speaking English and I just couldn't get the words out.

_____ e. I didn't have enough ideas.

_____ f. I had to think too much about trying to use the phrases.

_____ g. I felt nervous or shy.

_____ h. I couldn't understand the other speakers.

_____ i. The other speakers didn't give me a chance to talk.

_____ j. The other speakers didn't say enough, and I couldn't just talk to myself.

_____ k. _____

_____ l. _____

5. How can you solve each of the problems that you checked?

_____

_____

6. Overall, how do you rate the discussion? Use the following scale to rate the discussion:

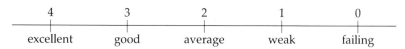

4	3	2	1	0
excellent	good	average	weak	failing

7. How do you think you can improve the next discussion?

_____

_____

Useful Vocabulary

This is a list of useful vocabulary words that appear in each section. You can go over the meanings of the words for each section immediately before covering that section of the unit. Some words may be listed more than once if they appear in different sections.

Listening Practice

Section 1 image
traditional
modern
to appeal to
advertising
to decrease
to increase

Section 2 merit pay bonus
productivity
to compete
conflict
stress

Controlled Practice

Exercise 1 advantage
disadvantage
to share

Exercise 2 goal
quality
productivity
to invest

to advertise
flexible
night shift
stock market

Exercise 3 brand
boss
to entertain
client
economical
stress
promotion

Communication Concepts

style
to communicate
formal
informal
neutral
acquaintance
colleague
subordinate
superior
favor
complaint

Role Playing

1A retired worker
retiree
financial
pension
inflation
budget
to improve
insurance
legal
counseling
fund
psychological
physical fitness
volunteer work

1B litter
media

lecture
seminar
recycling
container
wrapper
law
penalty
reward
campaign

1C   to control
to reduce
legal
to restrict
license
fine
inspection
advertising campaign
tax
car registration
fee
alternative
ride sharing

1D   nonunionized
absenteeism
tardiness
to complain
dissatisfaction
productivity
memo
flexible
facilities
in-service training
tuition
reward
working environment

Unit 2

Phrases

Suggesting action (including the speaker)
Let's _____.
Perhaps we could _____.
We might _____.
Why don't we _____?
Why not _____?
What about _____?
How about _____?
I suggest _____.

Accepting a suggestion
Yes, of course.
Certainly.
By all means.
Yes, that's a good idea.
Yes, why don't we try that?

Rejecting a suggestion
Unfortunately, _____.
I'm sorry, but _____.
Well, the problem is _____.
I'm not sure that will { be possible.
{ work.

Listening Practice

Section 1.   There is one short discussion in this section. Three partners are getting ready to open a new retail appliance store.

A.   Listen to the discussion. What is the purpose of this discussion?

Adv

_____

B.   Listen again. What suggestions do the speakers have? Make a list of the suggestions you hear.

Suggestion	*Phrase*
1. pay TV	why don't we
2. using radio comm	how about
3. ad local mag	why not
4. ad morning newspaper	Perhaps we could
5. posters	let's
6. check w/adv	I suggest

C.   Listen a third time. What phrases do the speakers use to introduce the suggestions? Write the phrase next to each suggestion in the list above.

Section 2.   There is one discussion in this section. An executive of a small bank is discussing a problem with two managers.

A.   Listen to the discussion. What is the problem they are discussing?

high turn over rate

_____

B.   Listen again as the suggestions are offered. Does the executive accept or reject the suggestions? Put a check [√] in the correct space.

Suggestion	*Accept*	*Reject*	*Phrase*
1. raise salaries	____	√	_____
2. give extra benefits	____	√	_____
3. show promotion opportunities	____	√	unfort

Suggestion	Accept	Reject	Phrase
4. talk to tellers individually	✓	___	*Yes that's*
5. stop requiring extra duties	✓	___	___
6. work on a questionnaire	___	✓	*Well*

C. Listen a third time. Write down the phrase in the list above that the speakers use to accept or reject the suggestions.

Controlled Practice

Exercise 1. Try to use some different phrases from the unit in discussing the illustrations on the following page.

> *Speaker A:* Make a suggestion based on each picture.

> *Speaker B:* Accept or reject the suggestion.

Exercise 2. Try to use a variety of phrases from the unit in discussing the following situations.

> *Student A:* Make a suggestion to deal with the situation.

> *Student B:* Accept or reject the suggestion. If you reject the suggestion, try to give a reason.

1. *(you to a colleague)* There is a lecture tomorrow night on computers. You are both interested in this subject.
2. *(a supervisor to another supervisor)* A lot of office supplies have been disappearing lately.
3. *(you to a colleague)* The two of you made a serious error in a report and the manager hasn't noticed it yet.
4. *(a manager to a supervisor)* The employees are all worrying about a rumor that many of them are going to be laid off soon.
5. *(you to a colleague)* Your boss seems to be angry about something, but you don't know what the cause is.
6. *(the director to a manager)* There is a very high turnover rate in the department.
7. *(an executive to another executive)* Many employees are complaining about how hard it is for them to find a parking place near the office.

1. no room on the bus

2. an upset colleague

3. a bank robbery

4. no porter in sight

8. *(a manager to another manager)* There is too much work for one secretary to do.
9. *(a supervisor to another supervisor)* Several new employees are not following company rules.
10. *(you to another supervisor)* Some employees are always late.
11. *(a secretary to another secretary)* The company you work for is automating the office and you're both afraid that you'll lose your jobs.
12. *(you to your colleague)* You are both bored by your jobs.
13. *(an executive to another executive)* Customers have been complaining that the company doesn't pay attention to their complaints.
14. *(an executive to another executive)* You believe that some employees are not working enough hours under the new flexitime policy.
15. *(an executive to a store manager)* You believe that shoplifting is increasing in your store.
16. *(a manager to another manager)* You believe that the company is not treating women employees fairly.
17. *(you to a colleague)* You both are going on a business trip to Cairo for the first time and you don't know which hotel to stay in.
18. *(an executive to another executive)* Several excellent positions overseas are opening up in your company.
19. *(you to a colleague)* Two of your colleagues were fired today but nobody knows the cause.
20. *(an executive to another executive)* You both believe that a new drug your company produces has not been adequately tested for safety in children.
21. *(you to a colleague)* It's time to leave work, but you two still have several urgent matters to discuss.
22. *(an executive to another executive)* You both think that another executive [a friend] is stealing small amounts of money from your company.
23. *(you to a friend)* You are both having trouble quitting smoking.
24. *(you to a colleague)* You are both quite upset over putting in a lot of work and then losing an important contract.
25. *(an executive to another executive)* It's difficult to find out how employees feel about a recent policy change.

Exercise 3. Put yourselves into the following roles. Try to use a variety of phrases from the unit in discussing the following situations.

Student A: Make a suggestion based on the situation.

Student B: Accept or reject the suggestion.

Student C: Make another suggestion.

Student D: Accept or reject the suggestion.

1. *supervisors:* how to deal with an employee who wastes too much time talking with other employees
2. *city authorities:* how to persuade more people to use public transportation
3. *students:* how to improve English class
4. *managers:* how to decrease boredom on the production line
5. *business partners:* what to name their new hotel on a beach
6. *managers:* how to deal with a long-time secretary who has become quite careless in work habits and is rude to clients
7. *teachers:* how to make their students do their homework
8. *employees:* how they can save money
9. *store managers:* how to improve customer service
10. *managers:* how to improve meetings
11. *employees:* how to persuade the company to give them a raise
12. *company directors:* how to fight back against workers staging an illegal strike
13. *managers:* how to deal with employees who call in sick at least once a week
14. *bank tellers:* how to deal with rude customers
15. *company librarians:* how to convince executives to return borrowed books within a reasonable time
16. *company executives:* how to reward workers who contribute money-saving suggestions
17. *managers:* how to improve the employees' lounge
18. *citizens:* how to conserve electricity
19. *hotel executives:* how to promote their hotel to attract more guests
20. *company executives:* how to keep qualified workers who are taking better-paying jobs with a competing company

Communication Concepts

Effective Meetings

These are guidelines for more effective meetings:

1. All participants should be informed in advance of the time, place, and probable length of the meeting. This should be done in writing, if possible.

2. A written agenda is useful if there are several points to be discussed. This agenda should clearly state the purpose of the meeting. If discussion group members have an agenda in advance, they will have a clear understanding of the topics and their order, and what the meeting will cover.

3. Even if an agenda is not provided, the group should have a specific purpose or goal to guide the discussion. Then all members take responsibility for accomplishing this goal.

4. Time limits for the meeting should be set up in advance. The meeting should start and end at the scheduled time.

5. Discussion group members should be present and ready to start on time.

6. Once the meeting starts, participants should not leave except for an emergency. Other participants may feel annoyed if people leave for routine matters such as making telephone calls or talking to visitors.

7. The meeting should be an honest, open exchange of ideas. This means that group members should expect and encourage differences of opinion. In fact, disagreements are useful since they help members look at different sides of an issue before making a decision. Members cannot learn from one another by agreeing all the time.

8. When participants are from different cultures, they should be especially careful that they understand each other. Silence, for example, may show agreement or it may show total disagreement. The word "yes" can mean that the person agrees, or it can mean simply that the person understands what is being said. Therefore, it may be necessary for members to ask more questions to make sure they understand what the others are thinking.

9. Discussion group members should consider the different ways of making a decision:
   a. Consensus: The members reach a general agreement through discussion.
   b. Voting:
      1) Majority vote: The members vote and the plan with more than half of the votes is selected.
      2) Plurality: If no plan receives more than half of the votes, the plan with the most votes is chosen.
   c. Authority: The leader or a strong member makes a decision.
   d. Default: The group is unable to reach a decision.

10. If possible, participants should try to reach a consensus. Clearly, the best decision is one that all members can agree on.

Discussion Techniques

Closing the Discussion

At the end of a discussion the group leader is in charge of closing the meeting. This closing should briefly cover the following points:

• *A statement that the meeting time is over*
"I'm afraid we'll have to end here. Unfortunately, we've run out of time."
"Excuse me, it looks like our time is up."
"I'm afraid that our time has run out."

• *A final summary of the discussion*
What conclusions were reached:

"To summarize, we $\left\{ \begin{array}{l} \text{agreed} \\ \text{decided} \end{array} \right\}$ that _____."

"In conclusion, _____."

     or

What was accomplished if no conclusions were reached:

"Well, we weren't able to come to an agreement, but I think that we accomplished a lot today."
"We haven't made a final decision yet, but we've made a lot of progress in exploring the issue."

• *A plan for a future meeting if the problem is not solved*
"We can discuss this further at our next meeting."
"Could we have a meeting soon to continue discussion of this subject?"

• *A statement to thank the members for their participation in the discussion*
"Thank you all for coming."
"I'd like to thank you all for your cooperation."

Role Playing

Organizing the Discussion

One way to help keep a discussion organized is to discuss one suggestion at a time. The suggestion should be analyzed to discover both its advantages and disadvantages. The following points are useful in evaluating possible solutions to a problem:

- Who will be responsible for putting the solution into effect?
- Will the solution really solve the problem?
- Is the solution economical? Will it cost much money?
- Does the solution affect productivity?
- How long will it take to get results? Will the solution solve the problem as soon as possible?
- How easy will the solution be to put into effect? That is, will it require making many changes, hiring new employees, training old employees, setting up new departments or offices, filling out reports, or organizing courses?
- Will the solution be acceptable to everyone involved?
- Is the solution fair to everyone involved?
- Is the solution legal?
- Will the solution cause new or different problems? If so, are these problems serious?
- How will the solution affect the morale of the people involved?

You should make these points into specific questions to fit each different solution. The type of questions you ask will depend on the type of solution that is offered. Of course, not all of the above points will apply to every solution.

Role Play 2A: Dealing with Extended Breaks

Situation

Supervisors in a manufacturing company have noticed that the employees are taking advantage of the break policy. The workers have two 15-minute breaks per day. However, they have been stretching their breaks to last up to 25 or 30 minutes each. The workers complain that the factory work is so boring that they need longer breaks. Also, the snack bar is so far away that it takes too long to walk there and back. The supervisors say the company is losing hundreds of work hours per year and employees should not be paid for time they are not working. The plant manager has called a meeting to discuss this issue.

Purpose of the Discussion

The purpose of this discussion is for the group members to decide on the best way to deal with the problem of extended breaks.

Group Roles

Leader: the plant manager
Supervisor(s)
Representative(s) of the employees

Brainstorming

What are different ways to solve this problem? Brainstorm as many
ideas as possible. You can use the following list of general points to
help you think of specific solutions:

- rewards or incentives (bonuses? awards? praise?)
- punishment (reduced pay? warnings? firing employees? sus-
  pending employees?)
- alternatives (change length or number of breaks? move snack
  bar?)

Specific solutions:

1. _____
2. _____
3. _____
4. _____
5. _____
6. _____
7. _____
8. _____
9. _____
10. _____

Selecting Ideas

Consider the different ideas that you developed during the brainstorming session. Go back and select the best ideas for each role:

Supervisors | *Employees*

Starting the Discussion

Now you are ready to start the discussion. Your group should discuss the topic for ten minutes. Again, do not worry if you do not have enough time to reach a final decision. Think about analyzing one suggestion completely before going on to the next one.

Observing: Evaluating the Discussion

1. *Listening to the discussion*
   a. What is the purpose of this discussion? Be specific.

   _____

   _____

   b. As you listen to the discussion, make a list of the different solutions that the group members suggest.

   _____

   _____

_____

_____

_____

2. *Follow-up to the discussion*

Which of the solutions do *you* think is the best? Why?

_____

_____

3. *Rating the discussion*

Use the following scales to rate the discussion group:

Participation: Did all members take part equally?

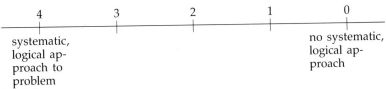

4	3	2	1	0

even spread;
equal partici-
pation by all

no spread

Problem Solving: Did the members work in a systematic, logical way toward agreeing on the best solution?

4	3	2	1	0

systematic,
logical ap-
proach to
problem
solving

no systematic,
logical ap-
proach

Role Play 2B: Organizing English Courses

Situation

New bank employees are required to study English if they don't pass a standard English test. The training department of the bank has organized these classes to run three hours per evening, five evenings a week for a 16-week semester. Representatives of the new employees have gone to the general manager to discuss this course. They complain that they can't be expected to work full-time and take 15 hours of class per week. This schedule is too demanding. The training department, however, says that this number of hours is necessary in order for the students to make good progress in a semester's time. Officials in the training department believe that it is not productive to have students study English for more than one or two semesters. The general manager has called a meeting to discuss this issue.

Purpose of the Discussion

The purpose of this discussion is for the group members to agree on the best way for the English courses to be organized.

Group Roles

Leader: the general manager
Representative(s) of the training department
Representative(s) of the new employees

Brainstorming

What are some different ways to solve this problem? Brainstorm as many ideas as possible. You can use the following list of general points to help you think of specific solutions:

- rewards and incentives (release time from work? increase in salary? pay bonus? promotion?)
- punishment (loss of job? cut in pay? loss of promotion possibilities?)
- alternatives (change schedule of classes? change job hours?)

Specific solutions:

1. _____
2. _____
3. _____
4. _____
5. _____
6. _____
7. _____
8. _____

9. _____

10. _____

Selecting Ideas

Consider the different ideas that you developed during the brainstorming session. Go back and select the best ideas for each role:

Training Department Representatives	*New Employees*

Starting the Discussion

Now you are ready to start the discussion. Your group should discuss the topic for ten minutes. Again, do not worry if you do not have enough time to reach a final decision. Think about analyzing one suggestion completely before going on to the next one.

Observing: Evaluating the Discussion

1. *Listening to the discussion*

a. What is the purpose of this discussion? Be specific.

_____

_____

b. As you listen to the discussion, make a list of the different solutions that the group members suggest.

_____

_____

_____

_____

_____

2. *Follow-up to the discussion*

Which of the solutions do *you* think is the best? Why?

_____

_____

3. *Rating the discussion*

Use the following scales to rate the discussion group:

Participation: Did all members take part equally?

4	3	2	1	0

even spread;
equal partici-
pation by all   no spread

Problem Solving: Did the members work in a systematic, logical way toward agreeing on the best solution?

4	3	2	1	0

systematic,
logical ap-
proach to
problem
solving   no systematic,
                                                 logical ap-
                                                 proach

Role Play 2C: Improving Women's Opportunities

Situation

Women employees in a bank are dissatisfied with their chances for promotion to executive-level positions. This bank employs almost 7,000 workers, over half of them women. However, only about 35 women (.5%) are in executive positions. This company, in fact, is typical of other companies in this country. The company often refuses to hire female college graduates because they are overeducated for the jobs that are open to them. Also, the company expects college-educated women to serve tea and perform clerical duties. Company executives believe that it is a waste of time and money to train women since two-thirds of them quit work after four or five years in order to get married. In this traditional culture, women are expected to get married and stay at home to care for their families. Women in this company, however, want to be given a fair chance to advance. If more of them are given equal opportunities, then more will continue to work after marriage. A group of women has asked the managing director to meet with them to discuss this issue.

Purpose of the Discussion

The purpose of this discussion is for the group members to decide what, if any, action should be taken by the bank to satisfy the demands of women employees.

Group Roles

Leader: the managing director
Representative(s) of the women employees
Representative(s) of the male executives

Brainstorming

What are different ways to solve this problem? Brainstorm as many ideas as possible. You can use the following list of general points to help you think of specific solutions:

- change attitude of male employees (in-company seminars? discussion groups? lectures?)
- train women for leadership positions (in-company courses? paid tuition for outside classes?)
- encourage women to continue working after marriage (rewards? flexible working hours?)
- allot a certain number of executive positions for women

Specific solutions:

1. _____

2. _____

3. _____

4. _____

5. _____

6. _____

7. _____

8. _____

9. _____

10. _____

Selecting Ideas

Consider the different ideas that you developed during the brainstorming session. Go back and select the best ideas for each role:

Women Employees	*Male Executives*

Starting the Discussion

Now you are ready to start the discussion. Your group should discuss the topic for ten minutes. Again, do not worry if you do not have enough time to reach a final decision. Think about analyzing one suggestion completely before going on to the next one.

Observing: Evaluating the Discussion

1. *Listening to the discussion*

   a. What is the purpose of this discussion? Be specific.

   _____

   _____

   b. As you listen to the discussion, make a list of the different solutions that the group members suggest.

   _____

   _____

   _____

   _____

   _____

2. *Follow-up to the discussion*

   Which of the solutions do *you* think is the best? Why?

   _____

   _____

3. *Rating the discussion*

   Use the following scales to rate the discussion group:

   Participation: Did all members take part equally?

4	3	2	1	0
even spread; equal participation by all				no spread

Problem Solving: Did the members work in a systematic, logical way toward agreeing on the best solution?

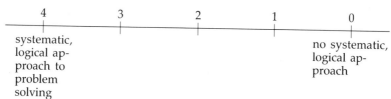

Role Play 2D: Solving a Smoking Problem

Situation

Several employees in an office have gone to the manager to complain. These non-smokers are bothered by the cigarette smoke in the office. Since the office is large and open, with about 35 employees, the non-smokers cannot escape from the smoke. These employees say that they suffer from watery eyes and headaches. One of the non-smokers, in fact, is allergic to cigarette smoke. The manager knows that many of the smokers would find it very difficult to work without being allowed to smoke. The manager has called a meeting to discuss this issue.

Purpose of the Discussion

The purpose of this discussion is for the group members to agree on a smoking policy for the office.

Group Roles

Leader: the office manager
Smoker(s)
Non-smoker(s)

Brainstorming

What are different ways to solve this problem? Brainstorm as many ideas as possible. You can use the following list of general points to help you think of specific solutions:

- education (in-company anti-smoking courses, lectures, or seminars? health counseling?)
- rewards (bonuses to non-smokers?)
- punishment (forbid smoking? fire or suspend employees who smoke in the office?)
- alternatives (separate smokers from non-smokers? majority vote to allow or forbid smoking in the office?)

Specific solutions:

1. _____
2. _____
3. _____
4. _____
5. _____
6. _____
7. _____
8. _____
9. _____
10. _____

Selecting Ideas

Consider the different ideas that you developed during the brainstorming session. Go back and select the best ideas for each role:

Smokers	*Non-smokers*

Smokers   *Non-smokers*

Starting the Discussion

Now you are ready to start the discussion. Your group should discuss the topic for ten minutes. Again, do not worry if you do not have enough time to reach a final decision. Think about analyzing one suggestion completely before going on to the next one.

Observing: Evaluating the Discussion

1. *Listening to the discussion*

  a. What is the purpose of this discussion? Be specific.

  _____

  _____

  b. As you listen to the discussion, make a list of the different solutions that the group members suggest.

  _____

  _____

  _____

  _____

  _____

2. *Follow-up to the discussion*

  Which of the solutions do *you* think is the best? Why?

  _____

  _____

3. *Rating the discussion*

Use the following scales to rate the discussion group:

Participation: Did all members take part equally?

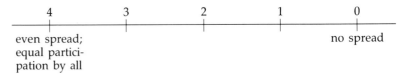

4	3	2	1	0
even spread; equal partici- pation by all				no spread

Problem Solving: Did the members work in a systematic, logical way toward agreeing on the best solution?

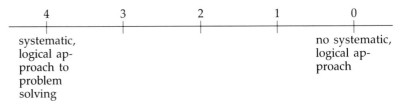

4	3	2	1	0
systematic, logical ap- proach to problem solving				no systematic, logical ap- proach

Useful Vocabulary

Listening Practice

Section 1   partner
retail
appliance

Section 2   opportunity
teller
individually
questionnaire

Controlled Practice

Exercise 2   lecture
office supplies
error
rumor
to be laid off
turnover rate
to automate
bored
flexitime

shoplifting
to be fired
urgent
to quit
upset
contract
policy

Exercise 3 to waste time
public transportation
partner
rude
client
to reward
to contribute
to conserve
to promote
to attract
qualified

Communication Concepts

participant
agenda
responsibility
emergency
annoyed
consensus
majority
plurality
authority
default

Role Playing

2A to deal with
to extend
to take advantage of
to stretch
snack bar
incentive
award
praise
warning
to fire
to suspend

2B   to pass
schedule
demanding
productive
incentive
release time
to cut

2C   dissatisfied
typical
to refuse
overeducated
clerical duties
to quit
traditional culture
attitude
to allot

2D   to be bothered
to escape
to suffer from
allergic

Unit 3

Phrases

Advising (someone else to do something)
Perhaps you could _____.
Maybe you should _____.
You might _____.
Why don't you _____?
Why not _____?

I think you $\begin{Bmatrix} \text{should} \\ \text{shouldn't} \end{Bmatrix}$ _____.

You'd $\begin{Bmatrix} \text{better} \\ \text{better not} \end{Bmatrix}$ _____.

Accepting advice
Yes, that's a good idea.
Yes, I'll do that.
Okay, I'll try that.
Of course.

Refusing advice
Well, the problem is _____.

I'm not sure that $\begin{Bmatrix} \text{is such a good idea.} \\ \text{will work.} \\ \text{will help.} \\ \text{will be necessary.} \end{Bmatrix}$

I'm afraid that might not $\begin{Bmatrix} \text{work.} \\ \text{help.} \\ \text{be possible.} \end{Bmatrix}$

I'm afraid I can't.

I don't know $\begin{Bmatrix} \text{how} \\ \text{if} \end{Bmatrix}$ I can.

Showing doubt
    Well, . . . ummm . . . maybe . . .
    Well, . . . possibly . . .
    Yes, . . . perhaps . . .
    Well, I'm just not sure.
    I don't know . . .

Listening Practice

Section 1.   There are eight dialogs in this section. Each one is about a
different business situation.

A.   Listen to the dialogs on the cassette. After you listen to each one,
answer the question about the situation. Circle the letter of the correct
answer.

1. The woman's boss _____.
    a. doesn't pay her enough   b. gives her too much work

2. The man _____ the last flight to New York.
    a. took   b. missed

3. The woman _____.
    a. talks too much   b. can't do her work

4. The man's business has been a _____.
    a. success   b. failure

5. Management can't _____ the problem.
    a. agree on a solution to   b. find the reason for

6. The new sales reps did _____ than expected.
    a. worse   b. better

7. The deliveries of small parts have been _____.
    a. late   b. on time

8. The woman has known about the _____ for a long time.
    a. doctor's appointment   b. meeting

B.   Listen again. Does the second speaker accept or reject the advice?
Put a check [√] in the correct space.

        Accept   *Reject*   *Phrase*

    1. _____   _____   _____

    2. _____   _____   _____

	Accept	Reject	Phrase
3.	_____	_____	_____
4.	_____	_____	_____
5.	_____	_____	_____
6.	_____	_____	_____
7.	_____	_____	_____
8.	_____	_____	_____

C. Listen a third time. Write down the phrase the speaker uses to accept or reject the advice in the list above.

Section 2. There is one discussion in this section. An executive of a multinational corporation is being transferred overseas. He is talking to two other executives about something that is worrying him.

A. Listen to the discussion. What is the executive worried about?

_____

B. Listen again. What advice do the speakers give? Make a list of the different kinds of advice you hear.

	Advice	Phrase
1.	_____	_____
2.	_____	_____
3.	_____	_____
4.	_____	_____
5.	_____	_____
6.	_____	_____
7.	_____	_____
8.	_____	_____

C. Listen one more time. What phrases do the speakers use to introduce the advice? Write the phrase next to each piece of advice in the list above.

Controlled Practice

Exercise 1. Try to use some different phrases from the unit in discussing the illustrations on the following two pages.

>*Speaker A:* Ask for advice on how to entertain different people.
>
>*Speaker B:* Offer some advice.
>
>*Speaker C:* Accept, show doubt, or reject the advice.

Exercise 2. Try to use a variety of phrases from the unit in discussing the following situations.

>*Student A:* Explain the problem to Student B in your own words.
>
>*Student B:* Offer some useful advice.
>
>*Student A:* Accept, reject, or show doubt over accepting this advice.

1. You have an important meeting in an hour, but you have a terrible headache.
2. The personnel manager is waiting for you to sign a contract, but you don't understand some parts of it.
3. You need to speak English better in order to get a promotion.
4. A good friend wrote you a check for $500 to pay back a debt, but the check bounced.
5. You need to go overseas immediately on business, but your passport has expired.
6. You've lost all of your credit cards.
7. You want to sell your car, but there's something wrong with the engine.
8. You're under a lot of stress at work and you can't relax.
9. You don't have enough money this month to make your car payment.
10. Your family is complaining that you don't spend any time with them because you always have to work late and on weekends.
11. You've been wasting a lot of time at work because some colleagues often stop in to chat.
12. The bank refused to give you a loan because of your bad credit rating.
13. You're so disorganized that you can never find the papers that you need.
14. A nice but incompetent employee has asked you to write a letter of recommendation.

The best place to take out $\left\{\begin{array}{l}\text{a client} \\ \text{your boss} \\ \text{a colleague} \\ \text{your family} \\ \text{a friend}\end{array}\right.$

a party

a shopping center

a restaurant

an art gallery

a park

55

a sports event

a country drive

a ballet

56

15. Your company wants to transfer you to another country, but you don't want to leave the country you live in now.
16. You had a disagreement with your boss today.
17. The bank teller accidentally gave you too much money, but you didn't realize it until you got home.
18. The government says that you didn't pay enough income tax last year.
19. Your boss wants you to give a lecture at the conference, but you're afraid of speaking in public.
20. Your best friend wants you to hire her for a job in your department, but you don't think she's right for the job.

Exercise 3. Try to use a variety of phrases from the unit in discussing the following situations.

Student A: Offer the other person some advice.

Student B: Accept, reject, or show doubt over accepting this advice.

1. you to a colleague who got fired yesterday
2. an executive to a manager who too often takes two-hour lunch breaks
3. you to your colleague who is frustrated because the boss never listens to his [or her] ideas
4. a supervisor to another supervisor who is having trouble with an employee who constantly complains
5. a supervisor to an employee whose work is careless
6. you to your friend whose driver's license has expired
7. a supervisor to a talented employee who refuses to follow instructions
8. a manager to an employee who doesn't wear the right kind of clothes to the office
9. a supervisor to an employee whose work area is disorganized
10. an executive to an employee who is impatient for a salary increase
11. a boss to a secretary who is behind in his [or her] work
12. you to a colleague who is working too hard
13. an executive to a manager who hasn't completed an urgent report
14. a manager to a sales representative whose sales are down
15. you to a friend who is going for an important job interview
16. a manager to a bank teller who is $200 short at the end of the day
17. you to a colleague who has to give an important presentation at a meeting next week
18. you to a friend who is spending more money than he [or she] earns

19. you to a friend who has bought a defective tape recorder
20. you to a colleague who wants to invest in the stock market
21. a union representative to workers who are angry about their company's refusal to increase their wages
22. you to a friend whose car keeps breaking down
23. the manager to a sales clerk who never wants to help the customers
24. a supervisor to another supervisor who has made several serious mistakes lately
25. an executive to another executive who wants to buy a personal computer for home use

Communication Concepts

Effective Leadership

As a discussion group leader it is your job to begin and end the meeting on time. There are also other responsibilities that you should fulfill in order to be an effective leader:

1. Prepare an agenda for the meeting to give to the participants in advance, if possible. Since the agenda lists the order of the main points to be discussed, it will help guide the discussion.
2. If there is only one issue to discuss, you may feel that an agenda is not necessary. In this case, be sure to make the purpose of the meeting clear.
3. Keep the discussion on the subject. If participants start moving off the topic or bringing up irrelevant points, politely bring the discussion back to the subject.
4. Try to keep the discussion organized. Once a suggestion has been introduced, try to get the group to examine it carefully before moving on to the next point.
5. See that all members have an equal chance to participate. Bring in quiet members by asking them questions. Also, control people who talk too much or monopolize the discussion.
6. Make sure that personal conflicts do not get in the way of accomplishing the goal. Keep the discussion focused on the issues at hand, not on the personalities of the members involved.
7. Keep the discussion moving. You have to decide when conversation is useful and should be encouraged. But you also have to cut off conversation if members spend too much time on one point or start repeating the same ideas.
8. Summarize when needed and look for areas of agreement. You

can ask "Do we agree that _____?" or "Then we agree that _____?" Of course, you are looking for agreement, but you cannot force it.

9. Make sure that all participants understand the discussion. In order to do this, you may have to restate or explain certain points.
10. Be fair and objective in leading the discussion. You can put in your own ideas, but don't push them. Accept all ideas equally.
11. Since a leader's opinion can have a strong effect, don't take advantage of this power. One way to do this is by putting your ideas in the form of questions. For example, you can ask "What do you think about _____?" or "What about _____?"
12. Show an encouraging attitude toward all participants. Make them feel that their ideas and suggestions are important to the group.
13. At the end of the meeting summarize the group's decision. Make sure that all participants understand and agree with this decision.

Discussion Techniques

Bringing in Others

For effective communication to take place in a discussion, all of the participants need to express their ideas. To encourage group interaction, the leader or other group members should bring in people who are not participating or are participating only a little. Here are several ways to bring others into the discussion:

What do you $\begin{cases} \text{think?} \\ \text{suggest?} \\ \text{advise?} \end{cases}$

What's your opinion?

Do you have anything to $\begin{cases} \text{say?} \\ \text{add?} \end{cases}$

Role Playing

Role Play 3A: A Kidnapping

Situation

An executive of a multinational corporation has just been kidnapped. The kidnappers are demanding that the company pay $8 million in cash immediately or they will kill the executive. Since this company's profits were $50 million last year, it can afford to pay this amount. Furthermore, the executive is a wealthy man with a fortune of about $200 million. The executive's family wants the company to pay the entire amount of the ransom right away. The company executives, on the other hand, want to delay for a while in order to negotiate with the kidnappers. Another problem is that the government has learned of this kidnapping. As is usual in these cases, the government has ordered the company *not* to meet the demands of the kidnappers. The government believes that this policy will discourage future kidnappings. A government official has announced that the government will seize the assets of the company if the ransom is paid. The Chairman of the Board of Directors has called a meeting to discuss the issue.

Purpose of the Discussion

The purpose of this discussion is for group members to agree on the best way to deal with the kidnapping.

Group Roles

Leader: the Chairman of the Board of Directors
Family member(s) of the kidnapped executive
Company executive(s)

Brainstorming

What are different ways to deal with the problem? Brainstorm as many ideas as possible. Write down these ideas on a separate sheet of paper.

Selecting Ideas

Consider the different ideas that you developed during the brainstorming session. Go back and select the best ideas for each role. Write down these ideas on a separate sheet of paper.

Starting the Discussion

Now you are ready to start the discussion. Your group should discuss the topic for twelve minutes. Do not worry if you do not have enough time to reach a final decision.

Observing: Evaluating the Discussion

1. *Listening to the discussion*

As you listen to the discussion, make a list of the different solutions that the group members offer.

_____

_____

_____

_____

_____

2. *Follow-up to the discussion*

What do you think is the best way to deal with the kidnapping? Why?

_____

_____

3. *Rating the discussion*

Use the following scales to rate the discussion group:

Pace: Did the discussion move along at the right speed?

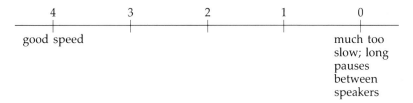

4	3	2	1	0
good speed				much too slow; long pauses between speakers

Leader Control: Did the leader effectively control the discussion?

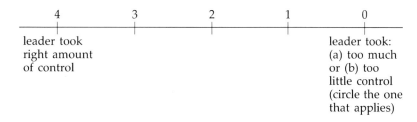

4	3	2	1	0
leader took right amount of control				leader took: (a) too much or (b) too little control (circle the one that applies)

Role Play 3B: Expanding Banking Services

Situation

A small bank with limited services is beginning to lose customers to larger banks. This bank offers customers checking and savings accounts, but no other special services. Larger banks, of course, offer a much wider range of customer services. The bank president wants to offer more services in order to keep and attract more customers. A meeting has been called to discuss this issue.

Purpose of the Discussion

The purpose of this discussion is for the group members to agree on which customer services to offer in order to keep and attract new customers.

Group Roles

Leader: the bank president
Customer representative(s)
Bank executive(s)

Brainstorming

What are different services that the bank might offer? Brainstorm as many ideas as possible. Write down these ideas on a separate sheet of paper.

Selecting Ideas

Consider the different ideas that you developed during the brainstorming session. Go back and select the best ideas for each role. Write down these ideas on a separate sheet of paper.

Starting the Discussion

Now you are ready to start the discussion. Your group should discuss the topic for twelve minutes. Do not worry if you do not have enough time to reach a final decision.

Observing: Evaluating the Discussion

1. *Listening to the discussion*

As you listen to the discussion, make a list of the different ideas that the group members discuss.

_____

_____

_____

_____

_____

2. *Follow-up to the discussion*

Which customer services do *you* think the bank should offer? Why?

_____

_____

3. *Rating the discussion*

Use the following scales to rate the discussion group:

Pace: Did the discussion move along at the right speed?

```
    4          3          2          1          0
 ___|_____|_____|_____|_____|___
  good speed                              much too
                                          slow; long
                                          pauses
                                          between
                                          speakers
```

Leader Control: Did the leader effectively control the discussion?

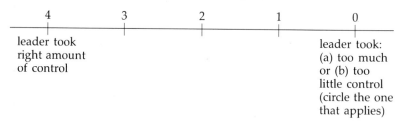

4	3	2	1	0
leader took right amount of control				leader took: (a) too much or (b) too little control (circle the one that applies)

Role Play 3C: Dealing with a Robbery

Situation

Two men tried to rob a pizza delivery man at knifepoint last week. Luckily, the delivery man was able to knock the knife away. He hit one of the robbers and broke his nose. Both of the robbers then ran away without the money.

Instead of praising the delivery man, the manager fired him. The manager did this because the company's policy clearly states that employees must always cooperate with robbers and immediately hand over money. The purpose of this policy is to prevent any employee from getting hurt. As the manager says, "Money can be replaced, but people cannot." The delivery man said that he knew about the policy. He added, though, that the robbers still could have hurt him even if he had given them the money.

A group of angry employees has gone to the owner of the company to complain about this decision. They want the delivery man rehired and given a reward. The owner has called a meeting to discuss this issue.

Purpose of the Discussion

The purpose of this discussion is for the group members to agree on the best way to handle this situation.

Group Roles

Leader: the company owner
The manager(s)
Representative(s) of the employees

Brainstorming

What are different ways of handling this situation? Brainstorm as many ideas as possible. Write down these ideas on a separate sheet of paper.

Selecting Ideas

Consider the different ideas that you developed during the brainstorming session. Go back and select the best ideas for each role. Write down these ideas on a separate sheet of paper.

Starting the Discussion

Now you are ready to start the discussion. Your group should discuss the topic for twelve minutes. Do not worry if you do not have enough time to reach a final decision.

Observing: Evaluating the Discussion

1. *Listening to the discussion*

   As you listen to the discussion, make a list of the main ideas that the group members present.

   _____

   _____

   _____

   _____

   _____

2. *Follow-up to the discussion*

   What do you think is the best way for the company to handle this situation? Why?

   _____

   _____

3. *Rating the discussion*

Use the following scales to rate the discussion group:

Pace: Did the discussion move along at the right speed?

| 4 | 3 | 2 | 1 | 0 |

good speed   much too
                                                  slow; long
                                                  pauses
                                                  between
                                                  speakers

Leader Control: Did the leader effectively control the discussion?

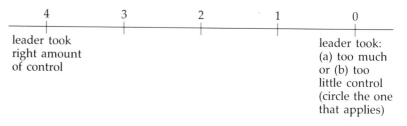

| 4 | 3 | 2 | 1 | 0 |

leader took   leader took:
right amount   (a) too much
of control   or (b) too
                                                 little control
                                                 (circle the one
                                                 that applies)

Role Play 3D: Hiring the Physically Handicapped

Situation

The personnel manager of a bank has recently refused to hire a job applicant who is physically handicapped. This person is a paraplegic (paralyzed in both legs). This applicant was well-qualified for the job he [or she] applied for, but the personnel manager decided to hire another equally qualified candidate. The manager said that there would be fewer problems hiring a person without a physical disability. Representatives of the handicapped applicant say that the company has a social responsibility to give handicapped workers a chance to work. The chief executive of the bank has agreed to a meeting to discuss this issue.

Purpose of the Discussion

The purpose of this discussion is for the group members to agree on a fair company policy regarding the hiring of handicapped people.

Group Roles

Leader: chief executive of the bank
Representative(s) of the handicapped applicant
Representative(s) of the personnel department

Brainstorming

What are different types of policies that the bank could have regarding the hiring of handicapped people? Brainstorm as many ideas as possible. Write down these ideas on a separate sheet of paper.

Selecting Ideas

Consider the different ideas that you developed during the brainstorming session. Go back and select the best ideas for each role. Write down these ideas on a separate sheet of paper.

Starting the Discussion

Now you are ready to start the discussion. Your group should discuss the topic for twelve minutes. Do not worry if you do not have enough time to reach a final decision.

Observing: Evaluating the Discussion

1. *Listening to the discussion*

As you listen to the discussion, make a list of the main arguments that the group members present.

_____

_____

_____

_____

_____

2. *Follow-up to the discussion*

What do *you* think is the best company policy regarding handicapped workers?

_____

_____

3. *Rating the discussion*

Use the following scales to rate the discussion group:

Pace: Did the discussion move along at the right speed?

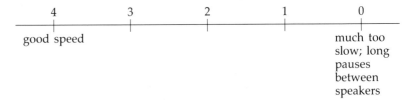

Leader Control: Did the leader effectively control the discussion?

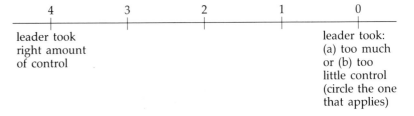

Useful Vocabulary

Listening Practice

Section 1   to miss
success
failure
sales rep
delivery

Section 2   multinational corporation
to be transferred
overseas

Controlled Practice

Exercise 2   to bounce
passport
to expire
credit card
to be under stress
to relax
to chat
loan
a bad credit rating
incompetent
letter of recommendation
to transfer
bank teller
income tax

Exercise 3   to get fired
frustrated
driver's license
to expire
impatient
defective

Communication Concepts

to fulfill
irrelevant point
to monopolize
conflict
to focus
personality
objective
to take advantage of

Role Playing

3A   to kidnap
profits
to afford
wealthy
ransom
to delay
to negotiate
policy
to seize the assets

3B	limited
	services
	customers
	checking account
	savings account
	to attract
3C	to rob
	to praise
	to fire
	policy
	to cooperate
	to prevent
	reward
3D	to refuse
	physically handicapped
	paraplegic
	well-qualified
	to apply for
	candidate
	disability
	social responsibility

Unit 4

Phrases

Requesting
Would you mind _____?
Could you please _____?
Do you think you could _____?
I wonder if you could [possibly] _____?
I'd really appreciate it if you could _____.

Agreeing to a request
Yes, of course.
Certainly.
By all means.

Refusing a request
I'm sorry, but _____.
I'm very sorry, but the problem is _____.
Unfortunately, _____.

Giving reasons
The reason is that _____.
This is because _____.

Listening Practice

Section 1. There are eight short dialogs in this section. Each one is about a different subject.

A. Listen to the dialogs on the cassette. After you listen to each one, write down where you think this conversation took place. For example, were the people in an office, in a hospital, or at a party?

Example: _____

1. _____   5. _____

2. _____   6. _____

3. _____   7. _____

4. _____   8. _____

B. Listen to the dialogs again. This time write down the phrase each speaker uses to make a request.

Example: _____

1. _____   5. _____

2. _____   6. _____

3. _____   7. _____

4. _____   8. _____

Section 2. There are eight short dialogs in this section. Each one is about a different office situation.

A. Listen to the dialogs on the cassette. After you listen to each one, decide whether the first speaker is requesting something from a colleague, a subordinate, or a superior. Put a check [√] in the correct space.

	Colleague	*Subordinate*	*Superior*
Example:	_____	_____	_____
1.	_____	_____	_____
2.	_____	_____	_____
3.	_____	_____	_____
4.	_____	_____	_____

	Colleague	Subordinate	Superior
5.	_____	_____	_____
6.	_____	_____	_____
7.	_____	_____	_____
8.	_____	_____	_____

B. Listen to the dialogs again. Decide whether the second speaker is agreeing to or refusing the request. Put a check [√] in the correct space.

	Agrees	Refuses
Example:	_____	_____
1.	_____	_____
2.	_____	_____
3.	_____	_____
4.	_____	_____
5.	_____	_____
6.	_____	_____
7.	_____	_____
8.	_____	_____

Section 3. There is one discussion in this section. The finance manager of a small company has to leave town unexpectedly on personal business. The manager is talking to two assistants.

Listen to the discussion on the cassette. What requests does the manager make?

1. _____

2. _____

3. _____

4. _____

5. _____

6. _____

Controlled Practice

Exercise 1. Try to use some different phrases from the unit in discussing the illustrations on the following page.

> *Speaker A:* Make a request based on each picture.
>
> *Speaker B:* Agree to or refuse the request.

Exercise 2. Try to use a variety of phrases from the unit in discussing the following situations.

> *Student A:* Make a request.
>
> *Student B:* Agree to or refuse the request. If you refuse, be sure to give a good reason.

1. The manager is talking to a secretary:
   a. The manager has misplaced an important file.
   b. An urgent letter must be sent out immediately.
   c. The manager needs five copies of a report.
   d. The manager doesn't want to be disturbed for the next half hour.
   e. The manager wants the secretary to stay late to do some extra typing.

2. An employee is talking to the manager:
   a. The employee wants to leave work early.
   b. The employee isn't going to finish the project on time.
   c. The employee wants to postpone a meeting with the manager until tomorrow.
   d. The employee would like a letter of recommendation.
   e. The employee needs a day off to take care of some personal business.

3. A secretary is talking to the manager:
   a. There are some letters that the manager must sign right away.
   b. The secretary feels that his [or her] lunch break is too short.
   c. The manager has given the secretary too much work to do to-day.
   d. The secretary wants to change the filing system.
   e. The secretary wants to hire an assistant.

4. An employee is talking to a colleague:
   a. The employee needs help with a project.
   b. The employee doesn't have enough money for lunch.
   c. One employee wants to read the other's newspaper.
   d. The employee needs a ride home.
   e. One employee doesn't understand what the other has just said.

1. trying to catch the elevator

2. trying to sit down

3. trying to stop someone
from smoking

4. trying to get change

5. The manager is talking to an employee:
  a. The employee often uses the photocopier for personal copying.
  b. The employee is often late to work.
  c. The employee is reading a magazine instead of working.
  d. The employee is playing loud music in the office.
  e. The employee is complaining to everyone (except the manager) that the manager treats him [or her] unfairly.

Exercise 3.   Try to use a variety of phrases from the unit in the following situations.

> *Student A:*   Make a request.
>
> *Student B:*   Agree to or refuse the request. If you refuse, be sure to give a good reason.

  1. *(recruit to manager)*   The new recruit doesn't understand what his [or her] job responsibilities are.
  2. *(employee to manager)*   The employee's child must go into the hospital tomorrow (a working day) for an operation.
  3. *(supervisor to employee)*   The employee's reports are not well organized.
  4. *(manager to employees)*   Weekly meetings never start on time because employees are late.
  5. *(employee to manager)*   The manager has assigned the employee to work on a project with someone he [or she] hates.
  6. *(manager to employee)*   The employee has not turned in monthly progress reports for the past two months.
  7. *(employee to a colleague)*   The colleague often talks so loudly that people in the office cannot concentrate on their work.
  8. *(director to manager)*   An urgent project is due tomorrow morning and it won't be ready by the end of the working day.
  9. *(you to a friend)*   Your friend keeps calling you at work to discuss private matters.
  10. *(you to a bank teller)*   You don't know what your bank balance is.
  11. *(you to a sales clerk)*   The coat you bought has a hole in it.
  12. *(you to a colleague)*   Smoke from your colleague's cigarette is bothering you.
  13. *(employee to manager)*   The employee suddenly feels very sick at work.
  14. *(you to a colleague)*   Your colleague often borrows your books without asking you.
  15. *(director to secretary)*   The letter is full of spelling mistakes.
  16. *(job applicant to secretary)*   The job applicant doesn't understand some of the questions on the job application.

17. *(director to manager)*   The director wants the manager's opinion on the new budget cuts.
18. *(discussion leader to a committee member)*   The leader wants someone to take notes of the meeting.
19. *(manager to employee)*   The employee has left work early for the past week.
20. *(employee to manager)*   The manager has just given the employee a job that the employee doesn't have time to do.
21. *(manager to supervisor)*   Several employees have complained that the supervisor has criticized them in front of other employees.
22. *(manager to employee)*   The employee went over the manager's head and complained to the director of the company.
23. *(manager to employee)*   The employee seems to be wasting a lot of time reading the newspaper.
24. *(you to a colleague)*   Your car is being repaired today and you need a ride to the garage.
25. *(interviewer to job applicant)*   The interviewer has some questions to ask the applicant.
26. *(employee to manager)*   Many employees are complaining about the bad condition of the employees' lounge.
27. *(manager to job applicant)*   The applicant has to fill out a job application.
28. *(you to a colleague)*   You have just told your colleague that you are quitting in a month but don't want anyone else to know yet.
29. *(director to manager)*   The director has an appointment with the manager, but an urgent problem has come up.
30. *(manager to employee)*   The employee has missed a week of work, but doesn't have a doctor's excuse.

Communication Concepts

Effective Participation

In order for you to be an effective participant in a group discussion, there are certain points that you should keep in mind:

1. Speak loudly and clearly enough for everyone to hear you. Also, use words that you know the others will understand or be ready to explain the meaning of any new or difficult words that you use.
2. Understand the goal of the discussion and be sure to keep all of your comments and questions on the subject.
3. Be prepared for the discussion. Study or collect all of the information you need in order to participate actively in the discussion.

4. Show initiative in the discussion. Don't wait for others to ask you questions before you make your comments. It is your responsibility to participate.
5. Listen carefully to the other members' ideas so that you can interact with them. You should examine their ideas by asking questions, getting further information, agreeing, and disagreeing. Be sure to ask questions if you don't understand what is going on.
6. Present your ideas as briefly as possible. This means that your comments should be short and to the point. It is usually more effective to make several brief remarks rather than one long statement.
7. If you have several important points to make, do not try to explain them all at once. The other members of the group will not be able to remember everything you have said. Thus, some of your points may be lost or ignored. It's better to make one strong point which the others can respond to and then put in your other points throughout the discussion.
8. Work as a member of a team. Present your ideas, but also bring in members who are quiet or shy. You must be willing to share speaking time and to consider opinions that are different from yours.
9. Be prepared to support your opinions with facts, reasons, and examples. Don't change your mind just because someone disagrees with you. Explain why you feel the way you do. Remember that a conflict of ideas within a group is useful since it helps the group to see different sides of an issue.
10. Keep an open mind. Once you've supported your opinion, be prepared to compromise or change your position if others present good strong arguments.

Discussion Techniques

Interrupting

Interrupting is a technique that should not be used very often since you want to let others finish their turn at speaking. Some speakers may speak quite slowly, but you have to be patient and allow them time to get their thoughts out. However, there are times when interrupting is appropriate. For example, if someone has been talking for some time, you may feel that you must get a point in. In this case, you can wait for a natural pause in the flow of speech—such as at the end of a sentence—and then say:

Excuse me, _____.

Excuse ⎰
Pardon ⎱ me for interrupting, but _____

Sorry to interrupt, but _____.

Role Playing

Role Play 4A: Food Poisoning

Situation

Thirty people have recently died from food poisoning. The victims, all from the same area, died after eating food prepared with flour made by a local company. Authorities have determined that the deaths are due to contaminated flour. The families of the victims are threatening to sue the company. The company has so far refused to accept responsibility for the deaths. A meeting has been called to discuss this issue.

Purpose of the Discussion

The purpose of this discussion is for the group members to agree on the best way for the company to deal with this problem.

Group Roles

Leader: a negotiator
Company representative(s)
Representative(s) of the victims' families

Preparing for the Discussion

Prepare for this discussion by brainstorming ideas and then selecting the best ideas to use.

Starting the Discussion

Your group should discuss the topic for fifteen minutes.

Observing: Evaluating an Individual

1. *Listening to an individual*

In this discussion you should observe only one speaker.

Speaker's name: ＿＿＿＿＿＿   Speaker's role: ＿＿＿＿＿＿

2. *Listening for content*

As you listen to the discussion, make a note of the ideas presented by the speaker.

＿＿＿＿＿＿＿＿＿＿＿＿＿＿＿＿＿＿＿＿＿＿＿＿＿＿＿＿＿＿＿＿

＿＿＿＿＿＿＿＿＿＿＿＿＿＿＿＿＿＿＿＿＿＿＿＿＿＿＿＿＿＿＿＿

＿＿＿＿＿＿＿＿＿＿＿＿＿＿＿＿＿＿＿＿＿＿＿＿＿＿＿＿＿＿＿＿

＿＿＿＿＿＿＿＿＿＿＿＿＿＿＿＿＿＿＿＿＿＿＿＿＿＿＿＿＿＿＿＿

＿＿＿＿＿＿＿＿＿＿＿＿＿＿＿＿＿＿＿＿＿＿＿＿＿＿＿＿＿＿＿＿

＿＿＿＿＿＿＿＿＿＿＿＿＿＿＿＿＿＿＿＿＿＿＿＿＿＿＿＿＿＿＿＿

3. *Evaluating content*

Put a check [√] in the appropriate space.

	Yes	Partially	No
a. Did the speaker talk loudly and clearly?	＿＿＿	＿＿＿	＿＿＿
b. Was the speaker easy to understand?	＿＿＿	＿＿＿	＿＿＿
c. Did the speaker show initiative?	＿＿＿	＿＿＿	＿＿＿
d. Were the speaker's comments brief and to the point?	＿＿＿	＿＿＿	＿＿＿
e. Did the speaker respond to others by asking questions, agreeing, or disagreeing?	＿＿＿	＿＿＿	＿＿＿
f. Did the speaker always stay on the subject?	＿＿＿	＿＿＿	＿＿＿

	Yes	Partially	No
g. Did the speaker speak about the right amount (not too much or too little)?	____	____	____

Role Play 4B: An Executive Shoplifter

Situation

A top-level executive of a major investment company has recently been caught shoplifting goods from a local department store. This is very hard to understand since the executive's salary is very high and the stolen goods were worth less than $100. In fact, the executive was accused of stealing some cassettes from a record store a few months ago, but most of the company executives considered the matter to be a terrible misunderstanding. Record store officials did not press charges because of the executive's excellent reputation. Now, however, the department store is planning to take legal action against the executive. The company president has called a meeting to discuss the issue.

Purpose of the Discussion

The purpose of this discussion is for the members to agree on the best way to handle the problem of the shoplifting executive.

Group Roles

Leader: the president of the investment company
Representative(s) of the shoplifting executive
Senior level executive(s) of the investment company
Department store representative(s)

Preparing for the Discussion

Prepare for this discussion by brainstorming ideas and then selecting the best ideas to use.

Starting the Discussion

Your group should discuss the topic for fifteen minutes.

Observing: Evaluating an Individual

1. *Listening to an individual*

   In this discussion you should observe only one speaker.

   Speaker's name: ——————— Speaker's role: ———————

2. *Listening for content*

   As you listen to the discussion, make a note of the ideas presented by the speaker.

   _____

   _____

   _____

   _____

   _____

   _____

3. *Evaluating content*

   Put a check [√] in the appropriate space.

	Yes	Partially	No
a. Did the speaker talk loudly and clearly?	———	———	———
b. Was the speaker easy to understand?	———	———	———
c. Did the speaker show initiative?	———	———	———
d. Were the speaker's comments brief and to the point?	———	———	———
e. Did the speaker respond to others by asking questions, agreeing, or disagreeing?	———	———	———

	Yes	Partially	No
f. Did the speaker always stay on the subject?	_____	_____	_____
g. Did the speaker speak about the right amount (not too much or too little)?	_____	_____	_____

Role Play 4C: An Extortion Note

Situation

A medium-sized company produces bottled fruit juices. The president of the company has just received an extortion note. This note said: "If you don't pay $500,000 immediately, we will put poison in bottles of your fruit juice." This letter contained 100 grams of cyanide poison to back up the threat. The company president doesn't know what to do. The production manager is worried about the possible consequences if the company doesn't make this threat public and then take all bottles of juice off the market. The finance manager, on the other hand, believes that the threat is probably false. If the threat is made public, the company will face almost certain ruin. The public will never again feel safe drinking the company's juices. The marketing manager thinks there might be further demands if the company agrees to pay the money now. The company president has called a meeting to discuss the problem.

Purpose of the Discussion

The purpose of this discussion is for the group members to agree on the best way to deal with this extortion note.

Group Roles

Leader: the president of the company
The production manager(s)
The finance manager(s)
The marketing manager(s)

Preparing for the Discussion

Prepare for this discussion by brainstorming ideas and then selecting the best ideas to use.

Starting the Discussion

Your group should discuss the topic for fifteen minutes.

Observing: Evaluating an Individual

1. *Listening to an individual*

   In this discussion you should observe only one speaker.

   Speaker's name: _____   Speaker's role: _____

2. *Listening for content*

   As you listen to the discussion, make a note of the ideas presented by the speaker.

   _____

   _____

   _____

   _____

   _____

   _____

3. *Evaluating content*

   Put a check [√] in the appropriate space.

	Yes	*Partially*	*No*
a. Did the speaker talk loudly and clearly?	_____	_____	_____
b. Was the speaker easy to understand?	_____	_____	_____
c. Did the speaker show initiative?	_____	_____	_____

	Yes	Partially	No
d. Were the speaker's comments brief and to the point?	_____	_____	_____
e. Did the speaker respond to others by asking questions, agreeing, or disagreeing?	_____	_____	_____
f. Did the speaker always stay on the subject?	_____	_____	_____
g. Did the speaker speak about the right amount (not too much or too little)?	_____	_____	_____

Role Play 4D: A Day Care Center

Situation

A large manufacturing company employs many workers with small children. Some of these parents have been having trouble finding someone to care for their children while they are at work. In order to solve this problem, a group of parents has asked the company to establish a day care center in the company. With reliable, affordable care for their children, parents say that absenteeism will be reduced and worker morale will be improved. The finance department is against this suggestion. A company day care center will cost a lot of money. In addition, it would not be fair to spend money on facilities that would not benefit all employees equally. The general manager has agreed to a meeting to discuss this issue.

Purpose of the Discussion

The purpose of this discussion is for the group members to decide what, if any, action the company should take to assist the parents with child care.

Group Roles

Leader: the general manager
Representative(s) of the parents
Representative(s) of the finance department

Preparing for the Discussion

Prepare for this discussion by brainstorming ideas and then selecting the best ideas to use.

Starting the Discussion

Your group should discuss the topic for fifteen minutes.

Observing: Evaluating an Individual

1. *Listening to an individual*

In this discussion you should observe only one speaker.

Speaker's name: _____   Speaker's role: _____

2. *Listening for content*

As you listen to the discussion, make a note of the ideas presented by the speaker.

_____

_____

_____

_____

_____

_____

3. *Evaluating content*

Put a check [√] in the appropriate space.

	Yes	Partially	No
a. Did the speaker talk loudly and clearly?	_____	_____	_____

	Yes	Partially	No
b. Was the speaker easy to understand?	_____	_____	_____
c. Did the speaker show initiative?	_____	_____	_____
d. Were the speaker's comments brief and to the point?	_____	_____	_____
e. Did the speaker respond to others by asking questions, agreeing, or disagreeing?	_____	_____	_____
f. Did the speaker always stay on the subject?	_____	_____	_____
g. Did the speaker speak about the right amount (not too much or too little)?	_____	_____	_____

Useful Vocabulary

Listening Practice
Section 3   finance manager
             assistant

Controlled Practice
Exercise 2   to misplace
              to be disturbed
              to postpone
              to sign
              photocopier

Exercise 3   recruit
              to assign
              progress report
              to concentrate
              bank balance
              job application
              to take notes
              to criticize
              to miss work

Communication Concepts
to show initiative
to examine
briefly
to respond
to share speaking time
a conflict of ideas
to support your opinion
to compromise

Role Playing
4A   food poisoning
victim
authorities
to determine
contaminated
to threaten
to sue
to accept responsibility

4B   investment company
to shoplift
department store
to accuse
to press charges
reputation

4C   extortion note
cyanide
to back up
threat
consequences
false
ruin
demand

4D   to establish
reliable
affordable
absenteeism
day care center
facilities
to benefit

Unit 5

Phrases

Stating a fact
Everyone knows that _____.
It's a fact that _____.

Note: Often there are no special phrases to introduce a statement of fact. A fact is something that everyone knows to be true. The following are examples of facts:

IBM manufactures computers.
This book is printed in English.
Hitachi Ltd. is based in Japan.
Kuwait is smaller than Saudi Arabia.

Refuting a fact
Actually, _____.
In fact, _____.
As a matter of fact, _____.
Well, I'm not really sure that's correct.
Are you sure? Isn't it true that _____?

Asking for information
Who _____?
Which _____?

What _____?
What kind of _____?
Where _____?
When _____?
Why _____?
How _____?
How often _____?
How much _____?
How many _____?
How long _____?

Listening Practice

Section 1. There are twelve short dialogs in this section.

Listen to the dialogs on the cassette. Decide whether the speakers are discussing facts or opinions. Put a check [√] in the correct space.

	Fact	Opinion		Fact	Opinion
Example:	_____	_____			
1.	_____	_____	7.	_____	_____
2.	_____	_____	8.	_____	_____
3.	_____	_____	9.	_____	_____
4.	_____	_____	10.	_____	_____
5.	_____	_____	11.	_____	_____
6.	_____	_____	12.	_____	_____

Section 2. There is one discussion in this section. The general manager is meeting with the head of personnel and the union leader.

A. Listen to the discussion on the cassette. What seems to be the major worry of the union leader?

_____

B. Listen again. What phrases do the speakers use to refute the following statements?

	Statement	*Phrase*
1.	Sales are down by 20%.	_____
2.	The company will be laying off workers soon.	_____
3.	The workers are going to be asked to take a 10% pay cut.	_____
4.	Five small companies have gone bankrupt.	_____
5.	The company will inform workers of any layoffs or pay cuts.	_____
6.	Several years ago the company laid off 50 workers with no notice.	_____

Controlled Practice

Exercise 1. Look at the income statement shown at the top of the following page. This is last year's income statement of a small company that manufactures shirts. Try to use some different phrases from the unit in discussing this statement.

Speaker A: Ask a question about this budget.

Speaker B: Answer the question, correctly or incorrectly.

Speaker C: Refute the statement if it is incorrect.

Exercise 2. The following are all statements of fact. However, they are incorrect statements. In discussing these statements, try to use a variety of phrases from the unit.

Student A: Make a statement.

Student B: Refute the statement and then give the correct information.

1. Part-time workers usually receive full benefits.
2. Singapore is a member of OPEC.
3. There are as many women as men in executive positions.
4. Property and buildings are examples of current assets.

SHIRTS UNLIMITED

STATEMENT OF INCOME   *Year ended December 31*

Net Sales $1,500,000

Costs and Expenses

    Materials   660,000
    Labor   320,500
    Marketing   80,000
    Shipping   18,000
    Management and office salaries   120,000
    Rent   48,750
    Utilities   21,225
    Depreciation   38,200
    Repairs   3,500
    Taxes, other than income taxes   28,300
    Estimated income taxes   140,000

        Total expenses   1,478,475

Net income for the year $21,525

---

5. The official language of Brazil is Spanish.
6. Jaguar automobiles are manufactured by a Japanese car company.
7. Lufthansa is a French airline company.
8. There is only one kind of computer language.
9. Advertising and marketing are the same thing.
10. A diskette is one kind of computer hardware.
11. Most large American companies offer guaranteed lifetime employment.
12. The purpose of recruitment is to decrease a company's work force.
13. Cash is a current liability.
14. A wholesaler always sells directly to the consumer.
15. An annual report is issued twice a year.
16. *The Wall Street Journal* is a famous book.
17. Japan is a member of the European Economic Community.
18. Consumer protection groups try to protect the interests of big business.

19. The currency used in India is called the yen.
20. Unions never bargain for fringe benefits for their workers.
21. If a company's expenses are more than its revenues, the company earns a profit.
22. Bangkok is located in Malaysia.
23. Life insurance generally covers all or part of hospital and medical expenses.
24. Import controls limit the number of goods that can be sold to foreign countries.
25. A multinational company invests in factories and equipment in only one country.
26. A short-term loan is usually due in ten years or more.
27. A corporation is owned by only one person.
28. Land is considered to be a liquid asset.
29. During a period of inflation, prices of goods usually decrease.
30. Pepsi and Coca-Cola are produced by the same company.

Exercise 3. Each of the following is a business problem with one possible solution. Students will ask different questions about each solution. Student A will answer each question with any suitable response. There is no one best answer.

Remember the different question words that you can use:

who, which, what, where, when, why, what kind of, how, how much, how many, how long, how often

Keep in mind the following points when thinking of questions. Make these points into specific questions to fit each solution. Not all the points will fit each solution.

- person or organization responsible?
- effective?
- cost?
- time?
- practical? easy to put into effect?
- acceptable to everyone?
- fair to everyone?
- new or different problems?

Student A: Explain the problem in your own words. Then offer the given solution.

Student B: Ask a question about the solution.

Student A: Answer the question with any suitable response.

Student C:	Ask another question.
Student A:	Answer the question.
Student D:	Ask another question.
Student A:	Answer the question.

1. *Problem:*   A company wants to help retired workers who say they feel useless.
  Solution: The company can hold social gatherings for the retirees.

2. *Problem:*   A manufacturing company wants to decrease absenteeism.
  Solution: The company can offer bonuses to workers who are never absent.

3. *Problem:*   A shop wants to attract more customers.
  Solution: The shop can have a big sale.

4. *Problem:*   Employees are stealing office supplies.
  Solution: The manager can send out a memo.

5. *Problem:*   Managers in a company write unclear, disorganized memos.
  Solution: The company can set up a training course.

6. *Problem:*   The government wants to persuade citizens to use less electricity.
  Solution: The leaders can organize a media campaign.

7. *Problem:*   A manager can't get work done because employees keep coming in to visit.
  Solution: The manager can arrange to see people by appointment only.

8. *Problem:*   A manager wants to improve communication within his [or her] department.
  Solution: The manager can set up meetings.

9. *Problem:*   Citizens in a country are taking advantage of the free public medical care.
  Solution: The country can introduce charges for health care.

10. *Problem:*   A small company wants to improve customer service.
  Solution: It can hire someone to be in charge of customer relations.

11. *Problem:*   The photocopier used by all the employees keeps breaking down.

Solution: The manager can allow only the secretary to use the machine.

12. Problem: Workers on a production line are complaining that they're bored.
Solution: The company can give them longer breaks.

13. Problem: A government agency has many incompetent workers.
Solution: The government can fire all of the incompetent people.

14. Problem: Students in a training course aren't doing their homework.
Solution: The instructor can send a memo to their managers.

15. Problem: People in the office are overworked and can't complete all of the necessary work.
Solution: The company can hire some part-time workers.

Exercise 4. Go back to the previous exercise. This time think of your own solution to each problem.

Student A: Explain the problem and then give you own solution.
Student B: Ask a question about the solution.
Student A: Answer the question.
Student C: Ask another question.
Student A: Answer the question.
Student D: Ask another question.
Student A: Answer the question.

Communication Concepts

Steps in Problem Solving

Making decisions in a group can become confusing if the group doesn't follow some kind of organized plan. Unfortunately, there is not one simple approach that will work for all kinds of problems. However, members of a group may be able to improve their decision-making skills by having a clear understanding of the most widely used approach to problem solving. This standard approach follows a problem–solution order. That is, the members of the group first analyze the problem and then move on to the solution stage of the discussion. This approach involves the following steps:

1. *Analyzing the problem*

   Once the leader has stated the problem, the group can begin to analyze it. The following points might be discussed:
   - What are the causes of the problem?
   - What are the effects of the problem?
   - What are the requirements of the best possible solution? (cost limits? time limits? acceptability to all members?)

   The purpose of this step is to bring out different viewpoints and facts so that everyone has a clear understanding of the problem.

2. *Suggesting solutions*

   Next, group members brainstorm a large number of possible solutions to the problem. During this brainstorming session members concentrate on developing all possible solutions without stopping to criticize any ideas. Then, once a list has been drawn up, the group can decide which solutions deserve serious consideration.

3. *Evaluating solutions*

   Now is the time for group members to discuss each of the proposed solutions in detail, one by one. The leader asks the member who suggested one of the ideas to explain it briefly. Then the other members interact by asking questions, getting further information, agreeing, and disagreeing. All of the members work together to bring out the possible advantages and disadvantages of this one solution. This is the time to decide whether the solution meets all of the requirements set up earlier during the problem analysis stage of the discussion. After the solution has been examined thoroughly, the leader can bring up another idea to discuss. Members should consider *all* of the proposed solutions before trying to make a final decision.

4. *Selecting the best solution*

   After all of the suggestions have been discussed, the group members can compare them. The members now have to decide which solution or combination of solutions has the most advantages and the fewest disadvantages. The group should try to reach a consensus on the best solution to the problem.

Discussion Techniques

Getting a Point into the Discussion

At times you may find it difficult to work your way into a discussion. There are some phrases, though, that you can use to get the attention of the other speakers before you make your point. The following are examples of attention-getting phrases used to introduce a comment or a question:

I have a $\left\{ \begin{array}{l} \text{suggestion} \\ \text{point} \end{array} \right\}$ I'd like to make.

I'd like to add something here.

I have a question I'd like to ask.

May I $\left\{ \begin{array}{l} \text{say} \\ \text{add} \\ \text{ask} \end{array} \right\}$ something?

Role Playing

Role Play 5A: Moonlighting

Situation

A large construction firm is considering prohibiting workers from moonlighting. *Moonlighting* is the practice of employees taking on second part-time jobs in addition to their full-time responsibilities. Officials from the personnel department say that moonlighting is interfering with the employees' efficiency. Studies have shown that accidents are most frequent on Mondays. This is partly because people who moonlight over the weekends are still tired. Furthermore, some workers have been calling in sick in order to work at their second jobs. Personnel department officials believe that moonlighters aren't devoting enough energy to their full-time jobs. Therefore, they want to dismiss any worker who is found moonlighting. Workers, however, argue that they have a right to work where and when they want to. Their salaries have not kept up with inflation. The personnel department has arranged a meeting with the company president.

Purpose of the Discussion

The purpose of this discussion is for the group members to agree on a fair policy regarding the practice of moonlighting.

Group Roles

Leader: the company president
Representative(s) of the personnel department
Representative(s) of the moonlighters

Observing: Evaluating an Individual

1. *Listening to an individual*

In this discussion you should observe only one speaker.

Speaker's name: _____ Speaker's role: _____

2. *Listening for functions*

Every time the speaker uses one of the following functions, put a check [√] in the appropriate space.

Function

a. Gives facts or opinions _____

b. Agrees _____

c. Disagrees _____

d. Suggests or advises _____

e. Asks questions _____

f. Other _____

3. *Evaluating the speaker*

After the discussion, use the following scales to rate the speaker:

Interaction: Did the speaker use many different functions?

4	3	2	1	0
excellent	good	average	weak	failing

Clear expression of ideas: Did the speaker clearly express his or her ideas?

4	3	2	1	0
excellent	good	average	weak	failing

4. *Making suggestions*

What suggestions can you give this speaker to help him [or her] improve?

_____

_____

Role Play 5B: Flexitime

Situation

The president of an insurance company is considering implementing a new policy of flexible working hours. This system of flexible working hours—flexitime—exists in many companies all over the world. With a flexitime policy, the workers can choose what time to begin and end work each day. However, they still work a set number of hours per week. Also, the workers may be required to be at work during a few key hours during the day, such as from 10:00 A.M. to 1:00 P.M. The workers support this flexitime policy because it gives them the right to choose convenient working hours. The managers, on the other hand, are worried that with a flexitime policy it will be impossible to supervise the employees properly. The president of the company has called a meeting to discuss this issue.

Purpose of the Discussion

The purpose of this discussion is for the group members to decide whether or not the company should implement a flexitime policy for all employees.

Group Roles

Leader: the president of the company
Representative(s) of the managers
Representative(s) of the employees

Observing: Evaluating an Individual

1. *Listening to an individual*

In this discussion you should observe only one speaker.

Speaker's name: _____ Speaker's role: _____

2. *Listening for functions*

Every time the speaker uses one of the following functions, put a check [√] in the appropriate space.

Function

a. Gives facts or opinions   _____

b. Agrees   _____

c. Disagrees   _____

d. Suggests or advises   _____

e. Asks questions   _____

f. Other   _____

3. *Evaluating the speaker*

After the discussion, use the following scales to rate the speaker:

Interaction: Did the speaker use many different functions?

4	3	2	1	0
excellent	good	average	weak	failing

Clear expression of ideas: Did the speaker clearly express his or her ideas?

4	3	2	1	0
excellent	good	average	weak	failing

4. *Making suggestions*

What suggestions can you give this speaker to help him [or her] improve?

_____

_____

Role Play 5C: A Compressed Work Week

Situation

A manufacturing company is considering putting into effect a compressed work week schedule. A compressed work week schedule means that the employees work ten hours per day for four days a week. This way they work a full number of hours per week, but they can also enjoy the benefits of a 3-day weekend. Most of the workers support this plan. The supervisors, however, are against this plan because they feel that it will result in lowered efficiency. The president of the company has called a meeting to discuss the issue.

Purpose of the Discussion

The purpose of this discussion is for the group members to decide what kind of work week schedule the company should adopt.

Group Roles

Leader: the president of the company
Representative(s) of the supervisors
Representative(s) of the employees

Observing: Evaluating an Individual

1. *Listening to an individual*

In this discussion you should observe only one speaker.

Speaker's name: _____ Speaker's role: _____

2. *Listening for functions*

Every time the speaker uses one of the following functions, put a check [√] in the appropriate space.

Function

a. Gives facts or opinions   _____

b. Agrees   _____

c. Disagrees   _____

      d. Suggests or advises   _____

      e. Asks questions   _____

      f. Other   _____

3. *Evaluating the speaker*

After the discussion, use the following scales to rate the speaker:

Interaction: Did the speaker use many different functions?

4	3	2	1	0
excellent	good	average	weak	failing

Clear expression of ideas: Did the speaker clearly express his or her ideas?

4	3	2	1	0
excellent	good	average	weak	failing

4. *Making suggestions*

What suggestions can you give this speaker to help him [or her] improve?

_____

_____

Role Play 5D: Disappearing Office Supplies

Situation

The finance department of a small company has recently sent a memo to the managing director. The finance department is concerned with the increasing amount of money being spent on office supplies, such as paper, pens, notebooks, folders, staplers and paper clips. In the past few months, expenditures for these office supplies have more than doubled.

    Up to now, the manager has informally allowed employees to take these supplies home for their personal use. In fact, the employees' wages are not very high and no raises are in sight. The manager feels that it has helped employee morale to let them take these supplies. Now, however, the situation has gotten out of control. The employees are taking home more supplies than they could possibly be using. The manager needs to take some action, but he [or she] doesn't want to cause bad feelings in the office. A meeting has been called to discuss the issue.

Purpose of the Discussion

The purpose of this discussion is for the group members to agree on the best way to handle this problem of disappearing office supplies.

Group Roles

Leader: the general manager
Representative(s) of the finance department
Representative(s) of the employees

Observing: Evaluating an Individual

1. *Listening to an individual*

In this discussion you should observe only one speaker.

Speaker's name: _____   Speaker's role: _____

2. *Listening for functions*

Every time the speaker uses one of the following functions, put a check [√] in the appropriate space.

Function

a. Gives facts or opinions   _____

b. Agrees   _____

c. Disagrees   _____

d. Suggests or advises   _____

e. Asks questions   _____

f. Other   _____

3. *Evaluating the speaker*

After the discussion, use the following scales to rate the speaker:

Interaction: Did the speaker use many different functions?

Clear expression of ideas: Did the speaker clearly express his or her ideas?

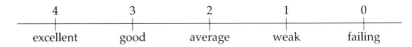

4. *Making suggestions*

What suggestions can you give this speaker to help him [or her] improve?

_____

_____

Halfway Point:
Participant Self-Evaluation

1. *Evaluate your own performance*

After you participate in a discussion, use the following scales to rate your own performance:

a. *Accuracy:* How well did you express yourself? How well did you use correct grammar and vocabulary?

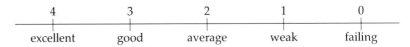

b. *Use of phrases:* Did you appropriately use a variety of phrases?

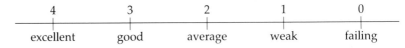

c. *Interaction:* Did you use many different functions?

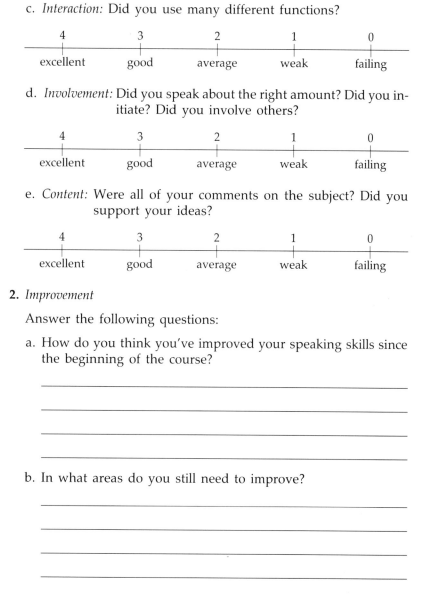

4	3	2	1	0
excellent	good	average	weak	failing

d. *Involvement:* Did you speak about the right amount? Did you initiate? Did you involve others?

4	3	2	1	0
excellent	good	average	weak	failing

e. *Content:* Were all of your comments on the subject? Did you
support your ideas?

4	3	2	1	0
excellent	good	average	weak	failing

2. *Improvement*

Answer the following questions:

a. How do you think you've improved your speaking skills since
the beginning of the course?

_____

_____

_____

_____

b. In what areas do you still need to improve?

_____

_____

_____

_____

Useful Vocabulary

Listening Practice
Section 2   general manager
head of personnel

union leader
to lay off
pay cut
to go bankrupt
to inform

Controlled Practice

Exercise 1   income statement
net sales
rent
utilities
depreciation
repairs
estimated
net income

Exercise 2   part-time workers
OPEC
property
current assets
diskette
computer hardware
current liability
wholesaler
currency
to bargain
fringe benefits
import controls
short-term loan
liquid asset
inflation

Exercise 3   to attract customers
memo
appointment
photocopier
incompetent

Communication Concepts

confusing
approach
to analyze
viewpoints
to concentrate

to develop
to criticize
to deserve
to evaluate
proposed
to reach a consensus

Role Playing

5A   to prohibit
        moonlighting
        to interfere with efficiency
        to devote energy
        to dismiss
        to argue
        inflation

5B   to implement a policy
        flexitime
        to support
        convenient

5C   to put into effect
        compressed work week
        to support
        efficiency

5D   folders
        staplers
        paper clips
        expenditures
        to allow
        wages
        morale
        to get out of control

Unit 6

Phrases

Getting further information
Would you mind explaining that a little more, please?
Could you tell us a bit more about that?
Could you please explain that in a little more detail?
Could you be more specific?

Asking for clarification
What do you mean?
Do you mean _____?
I don't quite follow.
I'm not sure what you mean.

Sorry, but I don't $\begin{Bmatrix} \text{understand} \\ \text{see} \end{Bmatrix}$ what you mean.

Clarifying your own ideas
I mean _____.
In other words, _____.
To put it another way, _____.
That is to say, _____.
What I mean is that _____.
The point I'm trying to make is _____.

108

Paraphrasing another person's ideas
  I think he [or she] means _____.
  What he [or she] means is that _____.
  In other words, he [or she] means _____.
  I think his [or her] point is that _____.

Listening Practice

Section 1.   There are eight dialogs in this section. Each one is about a different subject.

A.   Listen to the dialogs on the cassettes. Each dialog contains a new expression that is listed in this exercise. After you listen to each conversation, decide what the expression means. Circle the letter of the correct answer.

> *Example:*   *to be fed up with* means:
>   a. to be tired of doing something
>   b. to be interested in doing something

1. *to be as thick as thieves* means:
  a. to be friendly
  b. to be dishonest

2. *to hear something through the grapevine* means:
  a. to hear officially
  b. to hear unofficially

3. *to pull strings* means:
  a. to use hidden influence
  b. to do an excellent job

4. *to write off a debt* means:
  a. to collect it
  b. to cancel it

5. *to be out of your depth* means:
  a. you aren't qualified for the job
  b. you aren't happy with the job

6. *to play ball* means:
  a. to compete against
  b. to work with

7. *to pay through the nose* means:
a. to pay too much
b. to pay very little

8. *to lay your cards on the table* means:
a. to tell the truth
b. to take a break

B.   Listen again to the dialogs. How does the second speaker ask for clarification? Write down the phrase each speaker uses to ask for clarification.

Phrase

Example: _____

1. _____   5. _____

2. _____   6. _____

3. _____   7. _____

4. _____   8. _____

Section 2.   There is one discussion in this section. The personnel manager, general manager, and a supervisor are having a discussion.
Before you listen, look at the list of adjectives. How many of these words do you know? As you listen to the discussion, try to figure out the meanings of those words that you do not already know. Write down a general meaning of each of these words as you understand it from the discussion.

1. creative _____

2. arrogant _____

3. critical _____

4. straightforward _____

5. stubborn _____

6. competent _____

7. reliable _____

8. motivated _____

9. responsible _____

10. cooperative _____

Controlled Practice

Exercise 1. Look at the following advertisements. Try to use some different phrases from the unit in discussing these ads.

> *Speaker A:* Ask for clarification or get further information about the details of these ads.
>
> *Speaker B:* Clarify the point or give further information.

SALES MANAGER

Major international computer company seeks sales manager for challenging overseas position.

Applicant should have:

- a university degree in business or related field
- at least 8 years experience in computer sales, 4 at the management level
- overseas experience
- knowledge of at least 1 foreign language

Benefits include:

- competitive salary based on qualifications and experience
- excellent fringe benefits

Telephone: Barbara Carter, New York, at
            [800] 555-1324

ECONOMY Rent-a-Car

— *a wide range of models to choose from*
— *low rates*
— *self-drive and chauffeur driven cars*
— *fully comprehensive insurance*
— *unlimited mileage*
— *free delivery and collection*
— *excellent service*

For more details or reservations call: 391-9247

Exercise 2. Before going over this exercise in class, you may have to do some preparation. Try to find out what each of the following proverbs or sayings means. Then be able to explain it in your own words.

Student A:	Read the proverb.
Student B:	Ask for clarification.
Student A:	Clarify the meaning of the proverb.
Student B:	Ask for further information.
Student C:	Paraphrase what Student A said.

1. Birds of a feather flock together.
2. Too many cooks spoil the broth. —
3. Where there's a will there's a way.
4. When in Rome, do as the Romans do.
5. All that glitters is not gold.
6. A stitch in time saves nine.
7. Blood is thicker than water.
8. Don't make a mountain out of a molehill.
9. The early bird catches the worm.
10. Don't count your chickens before they're hatched.
11. People in glass houses shouldn't throw stones.
12. A bird in the hand is worth two in the bush.
13. Rome wasn't built in a day.
14. While the cat's away, the mice will play.
15. Don't put all your eggs in one basket.
16. Beggars can't be choosers.
17. A leopard can't change its spots.
18. You can't teach an old dog new tricks.
19. Two heads are better than one.
20. Don't cross a bridge until you come to it.
21. The grass is always greener on the other side of the fence.
22. Every cloud has a silver lining.
23. One man's meat is another man's poison.
24. Actions speak louder than words.
25. It's a dog-eat-dog world.

Exercise 3. You may have to prepare this exercise before going over it in class. Think of ways to complete the following sentences. Then be prepared to explain your ideas. Try to use a variety of phrases from the unit.

Student A:	Complete the sentence with an opinion.

Student B: Ask for clarification.
Student A: Clarify the statement.

1. Credit cards can _____.
2. A manager should _____.
3. Most labor unions _____.
4. Consumer complaints can _____.
5. Most employees oppose _____.
6. Working overtime _____.
7. Donating money to charity _____.
8. Many retired workers _____.
9. A good secretary should _____.
10. Employees are often frustrated when _____.
11. A supervisor can motivate workers by _____.
12. Learning English is _____.
13. Meetings often _____.
14. It's difficult for many executives to _____.
15. Multinational corporations _____.
16. Flexitime _____.
17. Advertising should _____.
18. The problem with computers is _____.
19. Working for a small company _____.
20. Luxury hotels _____.

Communication Concepts

Effective Listening

One advantage of making decisions in a small group is that the different members bring a variety of facts and opinions to contribute to the discussion. This advantage will be lost completely if the participants don't listen to and understand all of the ideas expressed by the group members. Thus, it is easy to see why effective listening is an essential skill in small group communication. By being a good listener, you encourage others to explain and develop their ideas. Furthermore, the best way to get others to listen carefully to your ideas is for you to listen to theirs.

One difficulty with listening comprehension is that many people have poor listening habits. For example, some people are more interested in talking than in listening. Others think about what they are going to say next rather than listening to what the speaker is saying. Another problem is that some people only listen to what interests them and don't bother to pay attention to anything else. In any case, good listening is a skill that can be improved by following these guidelines:

1. Concentrate on what the speaker is saying. Don't let your mind wander or think about other things while the speaker is talking.
2. Give the speaker all your attention. Don't take a lot of notes, look through papers or draw pictures.
3. Be patient. Let the speaker finish before you begin to speak. If you interrupt, the speaker may feel that you are not interested in what he [or she] has to say.
4. If you disagree with what the other person is saying, try to get a full understanding of that point of view before you speak. You may want to repeat the other person's idea to make sure that you understand it correctly.
5. If another person is making a point that you disagree with, do *not* plan what you are going to say while that speaker is still talking. If you are trying to think of what to say next, you cannot pay attention to the speaker's entire message.
6. Ask for clarification if you don't understand what the speaker has said. Also ask questions to encourage the speaker and show that you are listening.
7. Listen for the main ideas that the speaker is communicating. Examine the facts or details that the speaker uses to support the main ideas. Ask yourself whether these facts are relevant, reasonable, and support the speaker's arguments.
8. Try to judge what the speaker says rather than how well he [or she] says it. It is the content of the message that is important, not the delivery.
9. Use suitable body language to encourage other speakers—look interested in what they are saying, look directly at people when

they are speaking, and nod occasionally when you agree with them.

10. Keep an open mind and try to look at the situation from the other person's point of view. Try to show others that you are seriously considering their ideas.

Discussion Techniques

Avoiding Answering

There are times in a discussion when you are unwilling or unable to answer a question. It's possible that you don't have the necessary information or you simply don't have an opinion on the subject. If you don't say anything, it may seem that you haven't understood the question. Therefore, you can use one of the following phrases to show that you don't have an answer:

I'm afraid I $\left\{ \begin{array}{l} \text{don't know.} \\ \text{have no idea.} \end{array} \right.$

I don't really know.

I can't really say.

I don't think I can answer that.

It's $\left\{ \begin{array}{l} \text{difficult} \\ \text{impossible} \end{array} \right\}$ to say.

Perhaps someone else can answer that.

Role Playing

Role Play 6A: A 35-Hour Work Week

Situation

Unemployment is a serious problem in many countries. Labor unions in one country have an idea for reducing the number of unemployed workers. The union wants to reduce the 40-hour work week to 35 hours. Thus, more jobs will be created and the companies can hire more employees. The workers, of course, want to continue getting the same salary for less work. Company executives in this country, on the other hand, say that it's impossible for the workers to receive the same pay for shorter working hours. Also, the companies would have to pay out more in fringe benefits if additional workers were hired. A negotiator has been called in to lead a meeting to discuss this issue.

Purpose of the Discussion

The purpose of this discussion is for the group members to agree on the best way for them to work together in order to decrease unemployment.

Group Roles

Leader: a negotiator
Representative(s) of the unions
Representative(s) of different companies

Observing: Evaluating an Individual

1. *Listening to an individual*

In this discussion you should observe only one speaker.

Speaker's name: ⎯⎯⎯⎯⎯ Speaker's role: ⎯⎯⎯⎯⎯

2. *Listening for phrases*

Look at the following list of functions. Every time the speaker uses a phrase for one of these functions, write it down. Make a note if the phrase is used incorrectly or inappropriately.

Function	*Phrase*
a. Giving opinions	⎯⎯⎯⎯⎯⎯⎯⎯⎯⎯
b. Agreeing	⎯⎯⎯⎯⎯⎯⎯⎯⎯⎯
c. Disagreeing	⎯⎯⎯⎯⎯⎯⎯⎯⎯⎯
d. Suggesting or advising	⎯⎯⎯⎯⎯⎯⎯⎯⎯⎯
e. Requesting	⎯⎯⎯⎯⎯⎯⎯⎯⎯⎯
f. Refuting a fact	⎯⎯⎯⎯⎯⎯⎯⎯⎯⎯
g. Asking for information	⎯⎯⎯⎯⎯⎯⎯⎯⎯⎯

Function	Phrase
h. Asking for clarification	_____
i. Clarifying or paraphrasing	_____
j. Giving reasons	_____

3. *Evaluating the speaker*

After the discussion, use the following scale to rate the speaker:

Use of phrases: Did the speaker appropriately use a variety of phrases?

4	3	2	1	0
excellent	good	average	weak	failing

Role Play 6B: Flexiplace

Situation

Some employees at an insurance company have gone to the general manager to complain. They feel that they are under too much pressure to handle efficiently all of the paperwork in the office. They have suggested that the company implement a flexiplace policy. With a flexiplace plan, certain clerical and professional employees are allowed to work at home instead of at the office. This can be done by providing these workers with word processors or computer terminals that they can use at home. These are then linked to the company's office computer. The employees believe that flexiplace will reduce pressure since they will be able to work at their own speed. In addition, the company will require less office space, which will reduce overhead expenses. The supervisors, on the other hand, are afraid it will be difficult to supervise workers who are at home. Employees may not realize how difficult it will be to work at home since they can be distracted by home or family demands. The manager has called a meeting to discuss this issue.

Purpose of the Discussion

The purpose of this discussion is for the group members to decide whether the flexiplace plan is the best way to deal with the problem of so much paperwork.

Group Roles

Leader: the general manager
Representative(s) of the supervisors
Representative(s) of the employees

Observing: Evaluating an Individual

1. *Listening to an individual*

In this discussion you should observe only one speaker.

Speaker's name: _____ Speaker's role: _____

2. *Listening for phrases*

Look at the following list of functions. Every time the speaker uses a phrase for one of these functions, write it down. Make a note if the phrase is used incorrectly or inappropriately.

Function	*Phrase*
a. Giving opinions	_____
b. Agreeing	_____
c. Disagreeing	_____
d. Suggesting or advising	_____
e. Requesting	_____
f. Refuting a fact	_____
g. Asking for information	_____
h. Asking for clarification	_____
i. Clarifying or paraphrasing	_____
j. Giving reasons	_____

3. *Evaluating the speaker*

After the discussion, use the following scale to rate the speaker:

Use of phrases: Did the speaker appropriately use a variety of phrases?

4	3	2	1	0
excellent	good	average	weak	failing

Role Play 6C: Part-Time Workers

Situation

A department store employs many housewives as part-time workers. These workers receive a low hourly wage, and do not receive any of the benefits of the full-time workers. For example, they get no holiday pay, no sick leave, no health insurance, no bonuses, no pension plan, and no unemployment compensation. Many of these employees have been working at the store for many years and are efficient and reliable workers. A group of these part-time employees has asked the personnel manager to change their positions into permanent part-time jobs. This means that the workers will have job security plus the benefits of the full-time workers. At the same time, their schedules will still be flexible enough to allow them to take care of their family responsibilities. The personnel manager says that the store cannot afford the cost of these extra benefits. Also, if the store is going to pay out full benefits, it can just as easily hire full-time workers. The personnel manager has agreed to arrange a meeting with the general manager to discuss this issue.

Purpose of the Discussion

The purpose of this discussion is for the group members to decide what, if any, action should be taken to satisfy the demands of the part-time workers.

Group Roles

Leader: the general manager
Representative(s) of the personnel department
Representative(s) of the part-time workers

Observing: Evaluating an Individual

1. *Listening to an individual*

In this discussion you should observe only one speaker.

Speaker's name: _____ Speaker's role: _____

2. *Listening for phrases*

Look at the following list of functions. Every time the speaker uses a phrase for one of these functions, write it down. Make a note if the phrase is used incorrectly or inappropriately.

Function	*Phrase*
a. Giving opinions	_____
b. Agreeing	_____
c. Disagreeing	_____
d. Suggesting or advising	_____
e. Requesting	_____
f. Refuting a fact	_____
g. Asking for information	_____
h. Asking for clarification	_____
i. Clarifying or paraphrasing	_____
j. Giving reasons	_____

3. *Evaluating the speaker*

After the discussion, use the following scale to rate the speaker:

Use of phrases: Did the speaker appropriately use a variety of phrases?

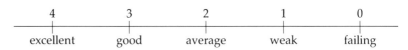

4	3	2	1	0
excellent	good	average	weak	failing

Role Play 6D: A Community Service Project

Situation

The management of a large computer company believes that the corporation has a responsibility to the community in which it does business. The company donates money to certain charities, but it is not directly involved in improving the quality of life in the community. Some companies encourage employees to get involved in community service programs by giving them the financial support and freedom to do so. This year the company's budget includes the sum of $100,000 to be spent on developing a community service project to help low-income families. The finance manager has called a meeting to discuss this issue.

Purpose of the Discussion

The purpose of this discussion is for the group members to agree on the best type of project to help low-income families.

Group Roles

Leader: the finance manager
Representative(s) of the employees
Representative(s) of low-income families

Observing: Evaluating an Individual

1. *Listening to an individual*

In this discussion you should observe only one speaker.

Speaker's name: _____   Speaker's role: _____

2. *Listening for phrases*

Look at the following list of functions. Every time the speaker uses a phrase for one of these functions, write it down. Make a note if the phrase is used incorrectly or inappropriately.

Function	*Phrase*
a. Giving opinions	_____
b. Agreeing	_____
c. Disagreeing	_____
d. Suggesting or advising	_____
e. Requesting	_____
f. Refuting a fact	_____
g. Asking for information	_____

Function	*Phrase*
h. Asking for clarification	_____
i. Clarifying or paraphrasing	_____
j. Giving reasons	_____

3. *Evaluating the speaker*

After the discussion, use the following scale to rate the speaker:

Use of phrases: Did the speaker appropriately use a variety of phrases?

4	3	2	1	0
excellent	good	average	weak	failing

Useful Vocabulary

Listening Practice
Section 2   adjectives

Controlled Practice
Exercise 1   to seek
chauffeur driven
comprehensive insurance

Exercise 2   feather
flock
broth
to glitter
molehill
worm
to hatch
stone
bush
beggar
leopard
cloud
lining

Exercise 3   labor unions
to donate
charity

frustrated
to motivate
multinational corporation

Communication Concepts

to contribute
essential
habits
to wander
patient
relevant
reasonable
to judge
content
suitable
body language
to nod

Role Playing

6A
to reduce
to create
fringe benefits
negotiator

6B
pressure
flexiplace
clerical employees
word processors
computer terminals
to link
overhead expenses
to be distracted

6C
department store
bonus
pension plan
unemployment compensation
efficient
reliable
job security

6D
responsibility
to donate
charity
community service project
low-income families

Unit 7

Phrases

Supporting an idea or suggestion

I think _____ is $\begin{Bmatrix} \text{a good} \\ \text{a great} \\ \text{an excellent} \end{Bmatrix}$ idea.

I'm for _____.
I'm in favor of _____.
I support _____.

The / One $\left\{ \text{main} \begin{Bmatrix} \text{advantage} \\ \text{benefit} \end{Bmatrix} \right\}$ of _____ is that _____.

Opposing an idea or suggestion

I think _____ is $\begin{Bmatrix} \text{not a good idea.} \\ \text{a waste of time.} \\ \text{a waste of money.} \end{Bmatrix}$

I'm against _____.
I'm not in favor of _____.

The / One $\left\{ \text{main} \begin{Bmatrix} \text{disadvantage of} \\ \text{drawback of} \\ \text{problem with} \end{Bmatrix} \right\}$ _____ is that _____.

124

Asking for examples
  For example?
  For instance?
  Such as?
  Could you give me an example?

Giving examples
  Let me give you an example.
  To give you an example, _____.
  For example, _____.
  For instance, _____.

Listening Practice

Section 1. There are ten short dialogs in this section. Each one is about a different subject.

A. Listen to the dialogs on the cassette. After you listen to each one, answer the question about what the first speaker said. Circle the letter of the correct answer.

1. The woman wants to spend _____ on advertising.
   a. more   b. less

2. The company is going to _____ using quality circles.
   a. try   b. stop

3. The company wants to choose someone who _____ currently working at the company.
   a. is   b. is not

4. The company will _____ workers to decrease absenteeism.
   a. reward   b. punish

5. The woman wants to spend _____ on office furniture.
   a. $10,000   b. $100,000

6. The man thinks they should have _____ prices.
   a. lower   b. higher

7. The woman wants to add _____ to the jobs.
   a. variety   b. difficulty

8. The man thinks the company should _____ money.
   a. borrow   b. loan

9. The store will offer _____ prices to certain customers.
    a. higher   b. lower

10. The man says that salaries should _____.
    a. decrease   b. increase

B. Listen to the dialogs again. Does the second speaker support or oppose the idea of the first speaker? Put a check [√] in the correct column.

	Support	*Oppose*		*Support*	*Oppose*
1.	_____	_____	**6.**	_____	_____
2.	_____	_____	**7.**	_____	_____
3.	_____	_____	**8.**	_____	_____
4.	_____	_____	**9.**	_____	_____
5.	_____	_____	**10.**	_____	_____

Section 2. There is one discussion in this section. A woman is talking to two friends.

A. What are some of the advantages and disadvantages of owning your own business? Before listening to the discussion, write down your own ideas in the chart.

OWNING YOUR OWN BUSINESS

Advantages	*Disadvantages*

B. Listen to the discussion. Check [√] the points you hear that are the same as the ones you've written down. Then add the other points that the speakers mention.

Controlled Practice

Exercise 1. Try to use some different phrases from the unit in discussing the illustrations on the following two pages.

> *Speaker A:* Explain a main advantage or a main disadvantage of each type of vacation.
>
> *Speaker B:* Agree or disagree, giving another advantage or disadvantage.

Exercise 2. Be sure that you understand all of the following terms before going over this exercise in class. Try to use a variety of phrases from the unit on these topics.

> *Student A:* Ask Student B's opinion on one of the following points.
>
> *Student B:* Support the idea and explain one advantage *or* oppose the idea and give a disadvantage.

1. merit pay bonuses
2. hiring handicapped workers
3. an income tax
4. banning video games in public
5. cigarette advertising
6. a 4-day work week
7. working on a commission basis
8. police going on strike
9. guaranteed lifetime employment
10. in-company day care centers
11. hiring relatives
12. 60 miles per hour [100 kilometers per hour] speed limits on highways
13. mandatory retirement
14. a flexitime policy
15. a 35-hour work week
16. promotion by seniority
17. job sharing
18. discriminating against foreign workers
19. a government anti-litter campaign

1. skiing

2. camping

3. staying at a resort

4. visiting a large city

5. taking a cruise

6. driving across country

7. seeing famous sights

8. staying with friends

129

20. banning smoking in public places
21. cheating on income tax
22. frequent meetings at work
23. free medical services
24. paying a ransom demand
25. giving part-time workers sick leave

Exercise 3.   Try to use a variety of phrases from the unit in the following exercise.

Student A: Make a general statement about each of these points, such as, "There are many _____."

Student B: Ask for examples.

Student A: Give a few examples.

1. types of taxes
2. computer companies
3. fringe benefits
4. ways to invest money
5. well-known proverbs
6. types of mass media
7. good programs on TV
8. computer languages
9. fixed costs of running a business
10. ways to advertise a new store
11. popular brands of stereos
12. good restaurants in town
13. ways to discipline a worker
14. types of luxury cars
15. widely-used credit cards
16. ways to relax
17. interesting ways to spend a vacation
18. famous hotel chains
19. well-known multinational companies
20. disadvantages of developing tourism in a country
21. types of insurance
22. services that a bank provides
23. good airlines
24. ways to cut costs in a factory
25. responsibilities of a manager

Communication Concepts

Group Task Roles

Discussion groups are formed for some purpose. This purpose is usually to perform a task such as solving a problem or making a decision. In order for the group to get its job done successfully, members must play different roles in the discussion. When members take on task roles they are helping the group accomplish its task. By understanding and performing these task roles, group members should be able to become more effective participants in a discussion. Here are some task roles that can be performed by the leader or any other members of the group:

1. *Initiating ideas or suggestions*

   Initiators suggest new ideas or actions. By bringing up new ideas for the group to discuss, initiators help the group to be more creative.

2. *Questioning*

   Questioners ask for facts, opinions, ideas, and suggestions from the other members. This helps group interaction and encourages other members to participate.

3. *Giving information or opinions*

   In this role, a member offers facts or opinions that are relevant to the problem being discussed.

4. *Clarifying ideas*

   Clarifiers work to clear up confusion. They may restate or explain unclear remarks to make sure that all members understand all the ideas.

5. *Evaluating*

   Evaluators judge the ideas and suggestions of the group to see how practical, economical, logical, or fair they are. Evaluators may try to explain the advantages or disadvantages of certain suggestions.

6. *Summarizing*

   Summarizers pull together and summarize the various ideas that have been offered. In trying to summarize, a member can check to see whether the group members have reached agreement on a particular point. In this way, a summarizer helps keep the group working toward the goal.

7. *Elaborating*

Elaborators give examples or further explanations of suggestions or ideas in order to show how they would work out if adopted by the group.

8. *Comparing*

A member may try to compare or show the relationships among various ideas that have been suggested by the group. This helps the members see which of the ideas is the best.

Discussion Techniques

Correcting Yourself

Sometimes you realize that another member of the discussion group has misunderstood or misinterpreted something you've said. It's also possible that you said something that you didn't really mean. For instance, you might have gotten your words mixed up or accidentally used a wrong word. In any case, you'll have to correct yourself to clear up any possible confusion. You can use one of the following phrases:

Actually, that's not what I $\begin{cases} \text{said.} \\ \text{meant.} \end{cases}$

I'm afraid you misunderstood me.

You must have misunderstood me.

Actually, what I $\begin{cases} \text{said} \\ \text{meant} \end{cases}$ was _____.

Role Playing

Role Play 7A: A Troubled Employee

Situation

A computer programmer has worked for a small company for about seven years. Up until six months ago, this employee was one of the hardest workers in the department. For the past six months, however, the employee has been going through a great deal of stress due to a serious illness in the family. For the first few months everyone in the office was very sympathetic. Since the man was clearly having severe emotional problems, the other workers divided up the work to cover for him. Now, though, these other computer programmers feel that enough is enough. They can't continue doing all this man's work for him. The serious illness could continue for many more months or even years. The man doesn't seem to be making any effort to take responsibility for his work. The supervisor is willing to let the situation continue as it is. This employee needs his salary. Also, he will be a good worker once this problem has passed. The manager is aware of the conflict in this department and has called a meeting to discuss the problem.

Purpose of the Discussion

The purpose of this discussion is for the group members to agree on the best way to deal with this troubled employee.

Group Roles

Leader: the manager
Representative(s) of the employees
The supervisor(s)

Observing: Evaluating the Discussion Process

1. As you observe the discussion, put a check [√] in the appropriate space. You may write more detailed comments in the space below each answer.

	Yes	Partially	No
a. Is the goal of the meeting clear?	_____	_____	_____
b. Do all members participate equally?	_____	_____	_____
c. Do all members stay on the topic?	_____	_____	_____

	Yes	Partially	No
d. Does the leader effectively guide the group?	_____	_____	_____
e. Does the discussion move in an organized way, not jumping from subject to subject?	_____	_____	_____
f. Is about the right amount of information covered in the time allotted (not too many different points or too few points discussed)?	_____	_____	_____

2. What suggestions can you make to help this group improve the next discussion?

_____

_____

Role Play 7B: Improving the Civil Service

Situation

Senior government officials are considering reforming the civil service. Up to now, government policy has made it practically impossible to dismiss any government employee. Government workers have been taking advantage of this situation. Although the official workday is seven hours long, studies show that working time is actually four and a half hours. Most employees arrive late, leave early, and take frequent coffee breaks. Many also leave to take care of personal errands, such as paying bills or picking up children from school. While in the office, many workers take naps, talk to friends on the telephone, or read the newspaper.

A group of consultants from the private sector has been called in by government officials to give suggestions for improving the current situation. Workers have been asked to attend the meeting to give their opinions on the suggestions.

Purpose of the Discussion

The purpose of this discussion is for the group members to agree on the best way to improve the efficiency of the civil service workers.

Group Roles

Leader: a senior government official
Representative(s) of the civil servants
Consultant(s) from the private sector

Observing: Evaluating the Discussion Process

1. As you observe the discussion, put a check [√] in the appropriate space. You may write more detailed comments in the space below each answer.

	Yes	*Partially*	*No*
a. Is the goal of the meeting clear?	_____	_____	_____
b. Do all members participate equally?	_____	_____	_____
c. Do all members stay on the topic?	_____	_____	_____
d. Does the leader effectively guide the group?	_____	_____	_____
e. Does the discussion move in an organized way, not jumping from subject to subject?	_____	_____	_____
f. Is about the right amount of information covered in the time allotted (not too many different points or too few points discussed)?	_____	_____	_____

2. What suggestions can you make to help this group improve the next discussion?

_____

_____

Role Play 7C: Job Sharing

Situation

A man and a woman who are married have applied for an executive position with a large multinational corporation. They are not competing for the same job, but they want to share it. This idea of job sharing has been gaining popularity in several countries, but it is still not a widespread practice. Under a job sharing system, two workers agree to divide the responsibilities of one full-time job. In addition to dividing the working hours in half, they also divide the salary and fringe benefits.

Both partners applying for this job are well-qualified for the position. They say that job sharing will make it possible for them both to spend more time with their children. The Director of Human Resources has discussed this job sharing idea with several company executives. Generally they are against the idea since they believe that it will be difficult to determine who is to blame for a bad decision. Also, they think that it will be harder to deal with two people instead of one. The applicants say, however, that the company will get two people for the price of one. In order to examine the idea further, the Director of Human Resources has asked for a meeting.

Purpose of the Discussion

The purpose of this discussion is for the group members to decide on a company policy regarding job sharing.

Group Roles

Leader: the Director of Human Resources
Company executive(s)
Representative(s) of the married couple

Observing: Evaluating the Discussion Process

1. As you observe the discussion, put a check [√] in the appropriate space. You may write more detailed comments in the space below each answer.

	Yes	Partially	No
a. Is the goal of the meeting clear?	_____	_____	_____
b. Do all members participate equally?	_____	_____	_____
c. Do all members stay on the topic?	_____	_____	_____
d. Does the leader effectively guide the group?	_____	_____	_____
e. Does the discussion move in an organized way, not jumping from subject to subject?	_____	_____	_____
f. Is about the right amount of information covered in the time allotted (not too many different points or too few points discussed)?	_____	_____	_____

2. What suggestions can you make to help this group improve the next discussion?

_____

_____

Role Play 7D: Producing Pesticide

Situation

A chemical company has been producing a certain pesticide for many years. This pesticide has been the company's main money maker for the past few years. However, a recent study by a researcher within the company has shown that this pesticide may cause cancer in rats. The researcher is afraid that the workers in the factory where this pesticide is manufactured may be exposing themselves to serious health dangers. Thus, the researcher wants to discontinue production immediately until further studies are more definite. The production manager, on the other hand, thinks that the company should continue production since stopping production could ruin the company and all the workers would then lose their jobs. Also, so far there is no proof that this pesticide is harmful to human beings. The chief executive of the company has called a meeting to discuss the issue.

Purpose of the Discussion

The purpose of this discussion is for the members of the group to decide what, if any, action should be taken in response to the researcher's findings.

Group Roles

Leader: the chief executive of the company
Researcher(s)
Production manager(s)

Observing: Evaluating the Discussion Process

1. As you observe the discussion, put a check [√] in the appropriate space. You may write more detailed comments in the space below each answer.

	Yes	Partially	No
a. Is the goal of the meeting clear?	_____	_____	_____
b. Do all members participate equally?	_____	_____	_____
c. Do all members stay on the topic?	_____	_____	_____
d. Does the leader effectively guide the group?	_____	_____	_____

	Yes	Partially	No
e. Does the discussion move in an organized way, not jumping from subject to subject?	_____	_____	_____
f. Is about the right amount of information covered in the time allotted (not too many different points or too few points discussed)?	_____	_____	_____

2. What suggestions can you make to help this group improve the next discussion?

_____

_____

Useful Vocabulary

Listening Practice
Section 1   quality circles

Controlled Practice
Exercise 1   resort
                cruise

Exercise 2   merit pay bonus
                handicapped worker
                to ban
                video game
                commission
                to go on strike
                guaranteed lifetime employment
                day care center
                mandatory retirement
                promotion by seniority
                job sharing
                to discriminate
                anti-litter campaign

to cheat
ransom demand
sick leave

Exercise 3   proverb
fixed cost
to discipline
hotel chain
multinational corporation

Communication Concepts
to accomplish a task
to perform a role
creative
relevant
logical
to adopt

Role Playing
7A   sympathetic
emotional problem
to cover for someone

7B   to reform
civil service
to dismiss
errand
nap
consultant
private sector
efficiency

7C   to compete
to gain popularity
a widespread practice
to determine
to blame

7D   pesticide
researcher
to expose
to discontinue production
proof

Unit 8

Phrases

Asking about preferences

Which $\left\{\begin{array}{l}\text{idea}\\\text{plan}\\\text{solution}\\\text{suggestion}\end{array}\right\}$ do you $\left\{\begin{array}{l}\text{think is better? (\textit{comparing two})}\\\text{like the most? (\textit{comparing three or more})}\\\text{prefer?}\end{array}\right.$

Comparing

This $\left\{\begin{array}{l}\text{idea}\\\text{plan}\\\text{solution}\\\text{suggestion}\end{array}\right\}$ is $\left\{\begin{array}{l}\text{better}\\\text{worse}\end{array}\right\}$ than that one. (*comparing two*)

This idea is more $\left\{\begin{array}{l}\text{practical}\\\text{effective}\\\text{useful}\\\text{beneficial}\\\text{economical}\end{array}\right\}$ than that one. (*comparing two*)

This idea is the $\left\{\begin{array}{l}\text{best}\\\text{worst}\end{array}\right\}$ one of all. (*comparing three or more*)

This idea is the most $\left\{\begin{array}{l}\text{practical}\\\text{effective}\\\text{useful}\\\text{beneficial}\\\text{economical}\end{array}\right\}$ of all. (*comparing three or more*)

Showing similarities

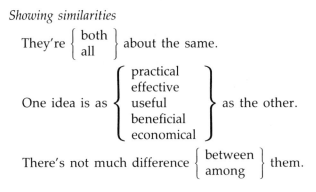

They're $\left\{ \begin{array}{l} \text{both} \\ \text{all} \end{array} \right\}$ about the same.

One idea is as $\left\{ \begin{array}{l} \text{practical} \\ \text{effective} \\ \text{useful} \\ \text{beneficial} \\ \text{economical} \end{array} \right\}$ as the other.

There's not much difference $\left\{ \begin{array}{l} \text{between} \\ \text{among} \end{array} \right\}$ them.

Listening Practice

Section 1.   There is one discussion in this section. Three friends have applied for executive positions with different electronics companies. They are comparing notes on two of these companies.

A.   Look over the chart. What kind of information do you need to fill it in? Now listen to the discussion. As you listen, fill in the required information. Put a check [√] in the appropriate space.

Which company . . .	*Fidelity*	*Universal*
1. has higher total revenues?	————	————
2. pays higher salaries?	————	————
3. has more fringe benefits?	————	————
4. has a higher turnover rate?	————	————
5. emphasizes cooperation?	————	————
6. emphasizes competition?	————	————
7. is likely to fire unproductive workers?	————	————
8. is likely to transfer unproductive workers?	————	————
9. often promotes from within?	————	————
10. hires managers from outside?	————	————

B. Which company would you prefer to work for? Why?

_____

_____

Section 2. There is one discussion in this section. Three people are comparing asset management accounts offered by three different investment companies.

A. Look over the chart. What information do you need to fill it in? Now, listen to the discussion. As you listen, fill in the chart.

	National	*Golden*	*United*
1. Amount of initial investment?	_____	_____	_____
2. Name of credit card?	_____	_____	_____
3. Amount of annual fee?	_____	_____	_____
4. Cancelled checks returned without charge?	_____	_____	_____
5. Start-up date of service?	_____	_____	_____
6. Discount on stock purchases?	_____	_____	_____

B. Which asset management account would you choose? Why?

_____

_____

Controlled Practice

Exercise 1. Try to use some different phrases from the unit in discussing the illustrations on the following two pages.

Speaker A: Ask about Speaker B's preference.

Speaker B: Give your preference and compare it to the others.

Office Machines
Points to compare: efficient? cheap? expensive? useful? good? up-to-date?
easy to use?

1. a manual typewriter

2. an electronic typewriter

3. a word processor

Offices

Points to compare: pleasant to work in? comfortable? modern? large? small?
interesting? impressive? charming? expensive to furnish?

1. traditional

2. high-tech

3. elegant

Exercise 2. Try to use a variety of phrases from the unit in discussing these situations.

> *Student A:* Ask Student B which of the following he [or she] prefers.
>
> *Student B:* Compare the two or three things (ideas, activities, or places) using one of the adjectives in italics. Then give a reason for your opinion.

1. *satisfying, worthwhile*
   working for the government; working for a private company

2. *effective, creative*
   TV advertising; radio advertising; newspaper advertising

3. *fast, efficient*
   word processors; typewriters

4. *economical, comfortable*
   a Honda; a Jaguar; a BMW

5. *exciting, appealing*
   working for a multinational company; working for a small local company

6. *profitable, flexible*
   full-time work; part-time work

7. *risky, rewarding*
   owning your own company; working for someone else

8. *easy, interesting*
   being a full-time student; working full-time

9. *good, expensive*
   a Timex watch; a Rolex watch; a Seiko watch

10. *appropriate, comfortable*
    wearing blue jeans to the office; wearing a suit to the office; wearing shorts to the office

11. *safe, easy*
    paying by cash; paying by check; paying by credit card

12. *difficult, enjoyable*
    being the leader of a discussion group; being a member of a discussion group

13. *productive, desirable*
    a 40-hour work week; a 35-hour work week

14. *creative, interesting*
    working as an executive; working as a factory worker

15. *expensive, fast*
    writing letters; calling long distance

16. *personal, effective*
    sending memos; talking face to face

17. *dependable, risky*
    working for a salary; working on commission

18. *creative, specialized*
    consumer goods advertising; industrial advertising

19. *cheap, luxurious*
    flying first class; flying economy class

20. *powerful, large*
    home computers; office computers

21. *large, dangerous*
    New York; Athens; Tokyo

22. *convenient, hard*
    working regular hours; working the night shift

23. *tiring, practical*
    driving to work; taking a bus; taking a taxi

24. *good, easy*
    reaching a decision by consensus; reaching a decision by taking a vote

25. *popular, interesting*
    soccer; basketball

Exercise 3.   Before going over this exercise in class, think of three different examples of the following things. Try to use a variety of phrases from the unit.

> *Student A:*   Ask Student B about his [or her] preference.
>
> *Student B:*   Compare the three things you have chosen.

Examples

1. cities   _____   _____   _____

2. brands of computers   _____   _____   _____

3. hotels   _____   _____   _____

4. types of investments   _____   _____   _____

5. credit cards   _____   _____   _____

Examples

6. airlines   _____   _____   _____

7. companies   _____   _____   _____

8. methods of adver-
   tising   _____   _____   _____

9. cars   _____   _____   _____

10. restaurants   _____   _____   _____

11. sports   _____   _____   _____

12. magazines   _____   _____   _____

Communication Concepts

Group Building Roles

As people try to solve a problem in a group they have to deal both with the problem and with the other members of the group. Task roles, which deal with *what* the group is doing, are clearly important. However, there are other important roles that have to do with *how* the members reach their goal. In order for a group to be effective, the members should feel good about working with each other and about participating in the group. When group interaction occurs in a supportive atmosphere, the members show respect for the ideas of others and do not feel hurt when others disagree with them. This attitude keeps communication open throughout the discussion. In fact, the success of a problem-solving group is affected by how well the members work together.

In order for the group to interact effectively, there are certain group building roles that should be performed by the members. These group building roles help them have a positive attitude toward their task and increase the members' motivation to participate actively in the group. In a successful group discussion all of the members should feel responsible for taking whatever role is necessary to keep the group interacting in a positive way. Here are some common group building roles:

1. *Encouraging*

   Members of a group can encourage others by giving them the feeling that their contributions are important to the success of the discussion. Encouragers offer praise and show an interest in the ideas and suggestions of the others.

2. *Gate keeping*

   Gate keepers help to organize the discussion so that everyone has a chance to speak. That is, they try to bring in quiet members and they also try to control members who talk too much. Gate keepers work to keep communication open.

3. *Harmonizing*

   Harmonizers try to act as peacemakers to solve conflicts or disagreements that occur between other group members. They may try to reduce the tension or stress of a difficult situation by joking or suggesting a break.

4. *Compromising*

   Compromisers try to help the group find acceptable solutions by offering to compromise. That is, compromisers may admit that they are in error or offer to change their position in order to go along with the other members.

5. *Coaching*

   Coaches try to help other members who are having trouble expressing their ideas. A coach might help a member who cannot think of the correct word to use.

Discussion Techniques

Keeping the Discussion Moving

It is usually the group leader's responsibility to keep the discussion moving. Of course, the leader must be careful not to cut off discussion of a point too soon. However, when group members start repeating the same ideas or it seems that the discussion is not getting anywhere, the leader should move the discussion on to the next point. Even if the members cannot reach agreement, discussion of a particular point should not go on too long. The following phrases can be used to keep the discussion moving:

I think we'd better go on to another point.

I think we've covered this point. Let's move on to something else.

Let's go on to the next point.

I think we've spent enough time on this point. Why don't we go on to another issue?

To bring up another point, _____.

Are there any more comments before we go on to the next point?

Role Playing

Role Play 8A: Executive Benefits

Situation

A large international company has always given very generous benefits to its senior executives. Now, however, the company has suffered severe financial losses. The president of the company has told the executives that they will have to give up some of their benefits. However, in order to show its concern, the company will try to keep three benefits that the executives feel are the most essential. A group of senior level executives has gotten together to decide which benefits to ask to keep:

_____ **1.** 6-month sabbaticals (at half pay) every 10 years
_____ **2.** free overseas villa accommodation for use during holidays
_____ **3.** free company cars and expenses
_____ **4.** memberships to athletic or sports clubs
_____ **5.** company credit cards for personal expenses (up to $500 a month)
_____ **6.** interest free loans up to $20,000
_____ **7.** extended vacations (up to two months)
_____ **8.** free medical care for the entire family
_____ **9.** generous pension plan on retirement (90% of salary)
_____ **10.** use of the company airplanes
_____ **11.** school fees for children up to the age of 18
_____ **12.** first class travel on all business trips
_____ **13.** yearly bonus of shares of stock in the company
_____ **14.** _____
_____ **15.** _____
_____ **16.** _____

Instructions

1. By yourself, rank the five most important benefits from 1 to 5. Put number 1 for the most important, number 2 for the next most important, and so forth to number 5. Please do *not* discuss your choices with other students.
2. Now get into a group of four or five students. Choose a group leader. As a group, rank the three most important benefits. Of course, the members of the group should try to reach a decision that is acceptable to all the group members. You have 15 minutes in which to make a decision. If your group cannot agree, then the group leader will have to make the final decision.
3. Turn to p. 154 to fill out the evaluation form.

Role Play 8B: Qualities of a Good Secretary

Situation

The personnel department of a multinational corporation is doing a study to determine which qualities executives look for in a private secretary. The department plans to use the results of this study to help them evaluate applicants for high-level secretarial positions. The personnel department has asked a committee of company executives to rank the following qualities:

_____ 1. good grammar and spelling
_____ 2. intelligence
_____ 3. capacity to accept responsibility
_____ 4. loyalty
_____ 5. ability to speak several languages
_____ 6. ability to get along with people
_____ 7. beauty
_____ 8. good sense of humor
_____ 9. ability to work under pressure
_____ 10. good typing and shorthand skills
_____ 11. good personality
_____ 12. willingness to work long hours
_____ 13. punctuality and regular attendance
_____ 14. ability to deal with people diplomatically

_____ **15.** ability to keep secrets
_____ **16.** _____
_____ **17.** _____
_____ **18.** _____

Instructions

1. By yourself, rank the five most important qualities from 1 to 5. Put number 1 for the most important, number 2 for the next most important, and so forth to number 5. Please do *not* discuss your choices with other students.
2. Now get into a group of four or five students. Choose a group leader. As a group, rank the four most important qualities. Of course, the members of the group should try to reach a decision that is acceptable to all the group members. You have 15 minutes in which to make a decision. If your group cannot agree, then the group leader will have to make the final decision.
3. Turn to p. 154 to fill out the evaluation form.

Role Play 8C: Promotion Criteria

Situation

The manager of a department wants to promote one of the production workers to the position of supervisor. He [or She] needs to replace the present supervisor who is quitting. Of course the manager wants to choose the best person for the job. The problem is that the company does not have any set criteria to help with this decision. The manager has asked for a meeting with other managers in the company. He [or She] wants to draw up a list of the most important criteria to consider when choosing an employee to promote.

The managers can choose the worker who:

_____ **1.** has the most seniority
_____ **2.** is the most popular with the other production workers
_____ **3.** is recommended by the supervisor who is quitting
_____ **4.** is the most intelligent
_____ **5.** has the best productivity record
_____ **6.** needs the pay raise the most
_____ **7.** has the most education

_____	**8.** puts in the most overtime
_____	**9.** is best liked by the manager
_____	**10.** has the greatest technical knowledge of his [or her] job
_____	**11.** is recommended by the other supervisors
_____	**12.** is a natural leader in informal activities
_____	**13.** has the best communication skills
_____	**14.** _____
_____	**15.** _____

Instructions

1. By yourself, rank the five most important criteria from 1 to 5. Put number 1 for the most important, number 2 for the next most important, and so forth to number 5. Please do *not* discuss your choices with other students.
2. Now get into a group of four or five students. Choose a group leader. As a group, rank the three most important criteria to consider when deciding which employee to promote. Of course, the members of the group should try to reach a decision that is acceptable to all the group members. You have 15 minutes in which to make a decision. If your group cannot agree, then the group leader will have to make the final decision.
3. Turn to p. 154 to fill out the evaluation form.

Role Play 8D: A Company Brochure

Situation

The marketing department of a large multinational company is responsible for writing a brochure to publicize the company. The purpose of this brochure is to appeal to prospective employees. The brochure should make this company sound like a great company to work for. Clearly, the brochure can't list all of the good qualities of the company. It will have to stress certain characteristics. Therefore, the marketing department has asked a committee of employees from the department of human resources to select the most important characteristics that the brochure should emphasize. The brochure will certainly mention good salaries and strong benefits, so these haven't been included in the list. Which characteristics should be chosen?

_____ 1. pleasant workplace
_____ 2. possibility of overseas transfers
_____ 3. open communication
_____ 4. physical fitness centers on premises
_____ 5. informal atmosphere
_____ 6. feeling that workers are part of a team
_____ 7. promotions from within the company
_____ 8. stress on quality
_____ 9. profit sharing program for employees
_____ 10. job security
_____ 11. staff encouraged to join community service projects
_____ 12. company training programs
_____ 13. atmosphere encouraging suggestions and complaints
_____ 14. company-owned vacation spots
_____ 15. _____
_____ 16. _____
_____ 17. _____

Instructions

1. By yourself, rank the five most important characteristics from 1 to 5. Put number 1 for the most important, number 2 for the next most important, and so forth to number 5. Please do *not* discuss your choices with other students.
2. Now get into a group of four or five students. Choose a group leader. As a group, rank the three most important characteristics. Of course, the members of the group should try to reach a decision that is acceptable to all group members. You have 15 minutes in which to make a decision. If your group cannot agree, then the group leader will have to make the final decision.
3. Fill out the following evaluation form.

Evaluating the Decision Making Process

A. *Evaluating your own group*

This time you should evaluate how your own group functioned. After you finish the discussion, answer the following questions individually.

1. Which of the criteria did you choose as number 1 when you decided by yourself?

   _____

2. Did you change your mind during the discussion? Why or why not?

   _____

3. Did any particular members influence your decision? How or why did they have this influence?

   _____

   _____

4. How many people first chose the number 1 criterion that was the same as the group's final number 1 criterion?

   _____

5. How was the leader chosen?

   _____ a. general agreement

   _____ b. voting

   _____ c. someone volunteered

   _____ d. _____

6. Do you think that this was the best way to choose a leader? Why or why not?

   _____

   _____

   _____

7. How did the group reach a decision?

   _____ a. Consensus: The group reached a general agreement.

   _____ b. Majority vote: The criterion with more than half of the votes won.

   _____ c. Plurality: Since no criterion received more than half the votes, the one with the most votes won.

   _____ d. Authority: The leader (or a strong member) pushed through a decision.

   _____ e. Default: The group couldn't reach a decision.

8. Were you satisfied with the way the decision was reached? Why or why not?

_____

_____

9. How do you think the decision making process in your group could have been improved?

_____

_____

_____

B. *Comparing answers*

After all the groups have completed their discussions, compare your answers to these questions.

Useful Vocabulary

Listening Practice

Section 1   electronics company
to emphasize
cooperation
unproductive

Section 2   asset management account
investment company
initial investment
annual fee
cancelled check
discount

Controlled Practice

Exercise 2 satisfying
worthwhile
efficient
appealing
profitable
risky
rewarding
appropriate
productive
desirable
dependable
effective

specialized
luxurious
convenient
practical

Communication Concepts

supportive atmosphere
to show respect
positive attitude
to increase motivation
peacemakers
to reduce tension
to joke
to compromise

Role Playing

8A   generous benefits
to suffer financial losses
to give up benefits
to show concern
sabbatical
villa accommodation
extended vacation
pension plan

8B   to evaluate
intelligence
loyalty
shorthand
punctuality
diplomatically

8C   to quit
criteria
seniority
technical knowledge
natural leader

8D   brochure
to publicize
prospective employee
to stress
characteristics
physical fitness
premises
profit sharing

Unit 9

Phrases

Asking about alternatives

What else can $\left\{ \begin{array}{l} \text{I} \\ \text{we} \end{array} \right\}$ do?

What other alternatives $\left\{ \begin{array}{l} \text{can you think of?} \\ \text{do you see?} \\ \text{are there?} \end{array} \right.$

Are there any other possibilities?

Asking about consequences

What $\left\{ \begin{array}{l} \text{will} \\ \text{might} \end{array} \right\}$ happen if $\left\{ \begin{array}{l} \text{I ask for a raise?} \\ \text{we have a meeting?} \\ \text{they fire the manager?} \end{array} \right.$

Predicting consequences

If $\left\{ \begin{array}{l} \text{I ask for a raise,} \\ \text{we have a meeting,} \\ \text{they fire the manager,} \end{array} \right\}$ then $\left\{ \begin{array}{l} \text{I might get it.} \\ \text{we can discuss the problem.} \\ \text{he will be very upset.} \end{array} \right.$

Expressing possibility

$\left. \begin{array}{l} \text{Perhaps} \\ \text{Maybe} \end{array} \right\{$ _____.

It's possible that _____.

I
You
He   { may
She   { might }   _____.
It   { could
They
We

Listening Practice

Section 1.   There are eight dialogs in this section. Each one is about a different subject.

A.   Look at the following actions. What might happen if these actions are carried out? Before listening to the dialogs, write down one possible consequence of each action. Write your answer on the first line after the letter "a".

Action	*Possible consequence*
1. if the work week changes from six to five days	**a.** _____
	b. _____
2. if a company introduces job rotation	**a.** _____
	b. _____
3. if the recession gets worse	**a.** _____
	b. _____
4. if our company introduces quality circles	**a.** _____
	b. _____
5. if our company continues to be late with deliveries	**a.** _____
	b. _____

Action		Possible consequence
6. if our company increases the prices of our products	**a.**	_____
	b.	_____
7. if we keep developing better ways of protecting our products from being counterfeited	**a.**	_____
	b.	_____
8. if we give our workers pay raises	**a.**	_____
	b.	_____

B. Now listen to the dialogs. If the speaker mentions the same consequence that you have written down, put a check [√] next to it. If the speaker presents a different idea, write it down after the letter "b".

Section 2. There is one discussion in this section. Several company executives are discussing ways of improving communication within the company.

A. Look at the following actions. What might be the possible consequences of these actions? Before listening to the discussion, write down one possible consequence. Write your answer after the letter "a".

Action		Possible consequence
1. if employees have to write down their suggestions	**a.**	_____
	b.	_____
2. if they have more meetings	**a.**	_____
	b.	_____
3. if the company doesn't acknowledge employee suggestions	**a.**	_____
	b.	_____

Action	Possible consequence
4. if the company rejects suggestions	**a.** _____ **b.** _____
5. if the company uses an employee's suggestion	**a.** _____ **b.** _____
6. if employees have bad news or complaints about the company	**a.** _____ **b.** _____
7. if the company organizes communications training for the managers	**a.** _____ **b.** _____
8. if employees see that the company pays attention to their ideas	**a.** _____ **b.** _____

B.   Now listen to the discussion. If the speaker mentions the same consequence that you have written down, put a check [√] next to it. If the speaker presents a different idea, write it down after the letter "b".

Controlled Practice

Exercise 1.   Try to use some different phrases from the unit in discussing the illustrations on the following page.

> *Speaker A:*   Ask how to solve the problem.
> *Speaker B:*   Suggest one solution.
> *Speaker A:*   Predict the consequences of this solution.
> *Speaker C:*   Suggest an alternative solution.
> *Speaker B:*   Predict the consequences.

1. pollution

2. unemployment

3. inadequate company parking

4. unmotivated employees

Exercise 2.   Try to use a variety of phrases from the unit to complete the following sentences.

Student A: Complete the sentence in an appropriate way.

Student B: Complete the sentence in a different way.

1. If the company transfers me to another city, _____.
2. I might get a promotion if _____.
3. If the secretary is late one more time, _____.
4. If our company implements a flexitime policy soon, _____.
5. Our meetings might be better if _____.
6. If I ask the boss for a raise, _____.
7. If I get an M.B.A. degree from the States, _____
8. Absenteeism in this company will decrease if _____.
9. If the instructor gives me too much homework, _____.
10. A union might go on strike if _____.
11. Employees will be more productive if _____.
12. The company will agree to a 35-hour work week if _____.
13. If I buy a home computer, _____.
14. I will waste less time at work if _____.
15. If I cheat on my income tax, _____.
16. If the company sends me to Paris on business, _____.
17. If the police go on strike, _____.
18. This store will please consumers if _____.
19. If the company hires more handicapped workers, _____.
20. Part-time workers might be happier if _____.
21. Students in this class will be pleased if _____.
22. If members of a discussion group start to argue, _____.
23. If I buy a new car, _____.
24. This city might be improved if _____.
25. If the company has to lay off a lot of workers, _____.
26. If I write a bad check, _____.
27. If I put all my money in a savings account, _____.
28. This company might go bankrupt if _____.
29. My boss will be angry at me if _____.
30. If the government increases taxes, _____.

Exercise 3.   The following are actions that might happen. Try to use a variety of phrases from the unit in completing these actions.

> *Student A:* Ask Student B about the possible consequences of the action. "What will [might] happen if _____?" or "What will you do if _____?"
>
> *Student B:* Predict the consequences or express a possibility.

1. *(you)* spend more money than you earn
2. *(a subordinate)* refuses to follow your instructions
3. *(a member)* talks too much during a discussion
4. *(you)* get a large bonus
5. *(the airline)* loses your luggage
6. *(you)* have to give a speech at a conference
7. *(a meeting)* lasts too long
8. *(your committee)* cannot agree on a solution
9. *(you)* get mugged on a business trip to a large city
10. *(you)* forget to attend an important meeting with the boss
11. *(a subordinate)* misses a lot of work without a good reason
12. *(you)* lose your job
13. *(you)* are rude to a colleague
14. *(you)* have to work with someone you hate
15. *(you)* miss several car payments
16. *(a colleague)* cheats on his [or her] expense account
17. *(your company)* decreases salaries
18. *(your instructor)* is late to class
19. *(your boss)* asks you to stay late to do some extra work
20. *(you)* take on a second job

Exercise 4. Try to use a variety of phrases from the unit in discussing the following situations.

> *Student A:* Explain the situation and suggest one way to deal with it.
>
> *Student B:* Ask another student about an alternative.
>
> *Student C:* Suggest another possibility.

1. A manager thinks that an employee is embezzling money.
2. Citizens want to do something to reduce industrial pollution in their city.
3. A company wants to encourage workers to stop smoking.
4. The government wants to stop people from littering.
5. An airline company wants to make travelers' trips easier and more pleasant.
6. A police department wants to improve its image in the community.

7. An executive discovers that a colleague is selling corporate secrets to a competitor.
8. A person buys a used car from a friend, and the car breaks down a week after it is purchased.
9. An executive is offered a desirable overseas transfer, but his [or her] family does not want to move.
10. A charitable organization (such as a cancer society) wants to increase donations.
11. A worker wants to stop wasting so much time with a talkative colleague.
12. A manager wants to fire a competent worker because of a personality conflict between them.
13. An executive is offered a large amount of money to sell company secrets to the competition.
14. A hospital wants to attract more patients in order to stop losing money.
15. Management wants to convince workers to take a cut in pay.
16. A bank teller wants to improve his [or her] chances for promotion.
17. People want to spend their free time in interesting ways.
18. A committee leader wants to improve meetings.
19. The instructor wants to improve English class.
20. A union wants to persuade management to meet their demands.
21. People want to cut down on personal expenditures.
22. Management wants to decrease the high turnover rate.
23. Someone wants to earn a lot of money in a short time.
24. The government wants to help poor people.
25. Students want to improve their vocabulary.
26. A manager wants to reward hard working employees.
27. Management wants to cut company expenses.
28. People need to be better listeners.
29. Management wants to motivate workers to increase their productivity.
30. Women are not getting the promotions they feel they deserve.

Communication Concepts

Individual Blocking Roles

People in groups have certain needs that they think can be satisfied by being a member of a group. Although the main objective of a group is to reach a decision, members of the group may also have personal goals in mind. For example, members may want to feel important, to have some power, to impress people, or to make friends. The group must meet some of these needs in order to encourage members to be productive. Effective groups solve problems and make decisions, but at the same time they must give satisfaction to individual members.

There are times when members are not working toward the goals of the group, but they are working to satisfy more personal needs. For instance, a person might be more interested in getting personal attention than in working for the general benefit of the group. Thus, by trying to find individual satisfaction, the member may block the progress of the group.

These individual roles can harm group functioning and lead to poor group decisions. If a member starts to slow the progress of the group by taking on a blocking role, the group members should do all they can to discourage such behavior. Sometimes it may help to discuss these problems after the discussion so that members can improve the quality of the next discussion. Here are some examples of individual blocking roles that members should *not* take on:

1. *Withdrawing*

   Withdrawers are physically present during the discussion, but they do not participate in the discussion unless other members force them to.

2. *Dominating*

   Dominators try to take over a discussion. They may talk a lot and try to monopolize the discussion. Also, dominators may try to push through their own ideas or suggestions.

3. *Being aggressive*

   Aggressors blame others for problems. They may also show anger against another member or against the group.

4. *Blocking communication*

   Blockers stop the group's progress by arguing too much on one point, talking abour irrelevant points, or rejecting others' ideas without any consideration. Also, blockers may not listen to other members since they feel that they already know everything. They won't change their minds even if strong reasons are presented.

5. *Getting special attention*

   Some members try to call special attention to themselves by talking loudly or by acting in an unusual manner.

6. *Joking*

Members may joke too much or in an inappropriate way. This stops serious work from getting done.

Discussion Techniques

Returning to the Subject

In a good discussion a speaker's comments should be relevant both to the general subject and to the specific point under discussion. If a speaker says something that is not related to the subject at hand, it is usually the group leader's responsibility to point this out. Of course, it is extremely important to do this in a polite way without suddenly cutting that person off. Here are some comments to bring the discussion back to the subject:

Yes, that's an interesting idea, but it raises a different point. Could we come back to it a bit later?

That's a good idea. Let's come back to it later once we've finished discussing _____.

I think that's a point worth discussing. However, let's see if anyone has anything to add here before we move on to a different subject.

That's an interesting point, but perhaps it's a bit off the subject. We're discussing _____.

Role Playing

Role Play 9A: Raising the Retirement Age

Situation

Because of low birth rates and higher life expectancies, many countries are faced with the problem of an increasing number of older citizens. With many workers retiring at an early age, the work force is declining. This "aging" of the population means that some changes are going to have to take place. The government of a country facing this problem is planning strong measures to keep its people active and working until old age. The government wants to raise the retirement age from the current 55 to the age of 65. Officials also want to give tax benefits to encourage people to work even after the age of 65.

Retirement benefits will begin when people reach 65 instead of the present 55.

Citizens' groups are protesting this plan. Workers contribute almost 20% of their salaries into the government's retirement fund. Therefore, citizens feel that the government is only interested in saving money. Also, many workers support the current early retirement policy since it opens up employment opportunities for the young.

The government has asked a visiting United Nations official to study the problem. A meeting has been called to discuss the issue.

Purpose of the Discussion

The purpose of this discussion is for the group members to agree on a fair retirement policy for the country's citizens.

Group Roles

Leader: the visiting United Nations official
Government representative(s)
Representative(s) of the citizens' groups

Observing: Evaluating Group Task Roles

1. *Listening for group task roles*

Which group members perform the following group task roles in the discussion? Make a note each time a speaker performs one of these tasks. (You may identify each speaker by a number rather than by writing out the entire name.)

Number   Speaker's name

1   _____

2   _____

3   _____

4   _____

5   _____

Task

a. Initiating ideas and
    suggestions   _____

b. Questioning   _____

c. Giving information
    and opinions   _____

d. Clarifying ideas   _____

e. Evaluating advantages
    and disadvantages   _____

f. Summarizing   _____

g. Elaborating reasons
    and examples   _____

h. Comparing ideas and
    suggestions   _____

2. *Evaluating group task roles*

Which speakers do you think were the most effective? Why?

_____

_____

_____

Role Play 9B: Losing Talented Employees

Situation

The president of a large company is very worried about 25 computer
software designers who have threatened to resign. These employees
complain that career advancement is too slow. Also, high achievers
are not financially rewarded since each employee gets the same pay
as another employee with the same seniority. These employees are
willing to trade guaranteed lifetime employment for high pay and fast
advancement. This is unusual in a country where companies have
traditionally been able to depend on corporate loyalty. This company
usually hires employees directly from college, trains them, and ex-

pects them to stay with the company until retirement. Employees are then sure of steady, if slow, advancement.

These computer software designers are some of the most creative and hard working employees in the company. The president certainly doesn't want to lose their services. He understands their need for job satisfaction, but he doesn't know whether it's possible to change traditional company policy. It is clear, however, that times are changing. The president has called a meeting to discuss the issue.

Purpose of the Discussion

The purpose of this discussion is for the group members to decide what, if any, action should be taken to satisfy these 25 employees.

Group Roles

Leader: the company president
Representative(s) of the 25 computer software designers
Representative(s) of senior level executives

Observing: Evaluating Group Task Roles

1. *Listening for group task roles*

   Which group members perform the following group task roles in the discussion? Make a note each time a speaker performs one of these tasks. (You may identify each speaker by a number rather than by writing out the entire name.)

   Number   Speaker's name

   1   _____

   2   _____

   3   _____

   4   _____

   5   _____

Task

a. Initiating ideas and
   suggestions
   _____

b. Questioning
   _____

c. Giving information
   and opinions
   _____

d. Clarifying ideas
   _____

e. Evaluating advantages
   and disadvantages
   _____

f. Summarizing
   _____

g. Elaborating reasons
   and examples
   _____

h. Comparing ideas and
   suggestions
   _____

2. *Evaluating group task roles*

Which speakers do you think were the most effective? Why?

_____

_____

_____

Role Play 9C: Introducing Health Charges

Situation

Government officials are considering a proposal to introduce charges
for medical treatment and medicine. Up until now, this country has
offered all citizens free health care. In the last three years, however,
spending on state health care has doubled. With the current recession, it has become necessary to reduce these expenditures. The quality of hospital care has declined since hospitals lack money and space
to treat patients. Furthermore, citizens have been taking advantage of
the fact that health care is free. Patients don't even use much of the
medicine they are given, and many people visit the hospital when

they aren't really sick. Officials believe that people will act more responsibly if they have to pay something.

Citizens' groups are protesting the idea of these health charges. They believe that all citizens have a right to free medical care. At the same time, they are interested in receiving high quality health care. Citizens think that the government can reduce its spending in other areas. Government officials have called a meeting to discuss this issue.

Purpose of the Discussion

The purpose of this discussion is for the group members to agree on the best way to provide quality medical care to the citizens.

Group Roles

Leader: a government official
Representative(s) of the hospitals
Representative(s) of the citizens' groups

Observing: Evaluating Group Task Roles

1. *Listening for group task roles*

Which group members perform the following group task roles in the discussion? Make a note each time a speaker performs one of these tasks. (You may identify each speaker by a number rather than by writing out the entire name.)

Number   Speaker's name

1   _____

2   _____

3   _____

4   _____

5   _____

Task

a. Initiating ideas and
    suggestions   _____

b. Questioning   _____

c. Giving information
    and opinions   _____

d. Clarifying ideas   _____

e. Evaluating advantages
    and disadvantages   _____

f. Summarizing   _____

g. Elaborating reasons
    and examples   _____

h. Comparing ideas and
    suggestions   _____

2. *Evaluating group task roles*

Which speakers do you think were the most effective? Why?

_____

_____

_____

Role Play 9D: Handling a "Bug" in the Office

Situation

Executives of a small but innovative computer company have been
holding secret meetings for months. They have been discussing the
design features of their new computer. Two days ago the president of
the company noticed a cleaner in the conference room at an unusual
time. After the cleaner left, the president checked the room and discovered a "bug" under the conference table. Now the president real-
izes that a competing company has been listening in on their secret
meetings. Yesterday, at lunch with company executives, the president explained what he [or she] had discovered. Some of the younger

employees suggested that they should pretend not to know that the bug is there and give misleading information to their competitors. Older executives, on the other hand, want to take legal action. They want to bring in a special investigator or the police to catch the cleaner. Then they want to take the other firm to court on grounds of industrial espionage. Thus, they may be able to win a large financial settlement. The president has called a meeting to discuss this issue. (The meeting will not be in the bugged conference room.)

Purpose of the Discussion

The purpose of this discussion is for the group members to agree on the best way to handle the discovery of the bug in the conference room.

Group Roles

Leader: the president of the company
Older executive(s)
Younger executive(s)

Observing: Evaluating Group Task Roles

1. *Listening for group task roles*

Which group members perform the following group task roles in the discussion? Make a note each time a speaker performs one of these tasks. (You may identify each speaker by a number rather than by writing out the entire name.)

Number *Speaker's name*

1 _____

2 _____

3 _____

4 _____

5 _____

Task

a. Initiating ideas and suggestions

_____

b. Questioning

_____

c. Giving information and opinions

_____

d. Clarifying ideas

_____

e. Evaluating advantages and disadvantages

_____

f. Summarizing

_____

g. Elaborating reasons and examples

_____

h. Comparing ideas and suggestions

_____

2. *Evaluating group task roles*

Which speakers do you think were the most effective? Why?

_____

_____

_____

Useful Vocabulary

Listening Practice

Section 1   job rotation
recession
quality circles
to protect
to counterfeit

Section 2   to acknowledge

Controlled Practice

Exercise 2   to implement
an M.B.A. degree
bad check
to go bankrupt

Exercise 3 to get mugged
  expense account

Exercise 4 to embezzle
  industrial pollution
  littering
  corporate secret
  charitable organization
  donation
  expenditure

Communication Concepts
  to impress people
  to block
  to withdraw
  to dominate
  aggressive
  to argue

Role Playing

9A birth rates
  high life expectancy
  measure
  tax benefit
  to protest
  to contribute
  retirement fund
  employment opportunities

9B computer software
  to resign
  career advancement
  high achiever
  corporate loyalty

9C proposal
  recession

9D innovative
  design features
  conference
  "bug"
  investigator
  industrial espionage
  financial settlement

Unit 10

Phrases

Persuading and convincing
You must admit that _____.
You have to agree that _____.
Don't forget that _____.
Let's not forget that _____.
Don't you $\left\{ \begin{array}{l} \text{agree} \\ \text{think} \end{array} \right\}$ that _____?

Counterarguing
Even so, _____.
But still, _____.
Still, _____.
Nevertheless, _____.
But then again, _____.
All the same, _____.
In any case, _____.
Anyway, _____.
Even if that is $\left\{ \begin{array}{l} \text{true} \\ \text{so} \end{array} \right\}$, _____.

Conceding
Yes, I'll go along with that.
I'll agree with you there.
I'm willing to go along with you.
In that case, _____.
Well, you've convinced me.

Listening Practice

Section 1. There is one discussion in this section. Three company executives are discussing the possibility of moving company headquarters out of the city to a small town named Lawton about 200 kilometers away.

A. What are some of the arguments for and against a company's moving its headquarters out of the city? Before listening to the discussion, write down your ideas in the chart.

Arguments for	*Arguments against*

B. Now listen to the discussion. Check the arguments you hear that are the same as the ones you've written. Then add any additional arguments that the speakers use.

C. Which phrases do the speakers use to persuade each other? Write them down in the order that you hear them.

1. _____

2. _____

3. _____

4. _____

5. _____

Section 2. There is one discussion in this section. A sales rep from a computer company is discussing the possibility of automating a small company. The sales rep is talking with the general manager and the personnel manager of the company.

A. What are some of the arguments for and against automating a company? Before listening to the discussion, write down your ideas in the chart.

Arguments for	*Arguments against*

B. Now listen to the discussion. Check the arguments you hear that are the same as the ones you've written. Then add any other arguments that the speakers use.

C. Which phrases do the men use to counterargue? Write these phrases down in the order that you hear them.

1. _____

2. _____

3. _____

4. _____

5. _____

6. _____

Controlled Practice

Exercise 1. You and your partner are getting ready to open your own small consulting firm. You are furnishing the office on a very limited budget, but you want to make a good impression on potential clients. Since your budget is so small, you are not able to buy everything that you need right away.

Try to use some different phrases from the unit in discussing the illustrations on the following two pages.

Speaker A: Try to persuade Speaker B to buy one of the items.

Speaker B: Counterargue.

Here is your office:

What should you buy?

1. desk and chair

2. office computer

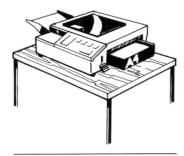

3. photocopier

4. sofa and chair

5. bookcase

6. plants

7. small refrigerator

8. automatic phone answering machine

Exercise 2. Try to use a variety of phrases from the unit in discussing the following situations.

> *Student A:* Tell Student B what you intend to do.
> *Student B:* Try to persuade Student B *not* to take that action.
> *Student A:* Counterargue.
> *Student B:* Try again to persuade Student A.
> *Student A:* Counterargue or concede.

1. You're going to quit your job.
2. You don't need a telephone. You're going to have your phone disconnected.
3. The sales clerk gave you too much money back, but you think you'll just keep it.
4. You're going to start smoking again.
5. You're going to sell your car and use public transportation from now on.
6. Getting a degree is a waste of time. You're going to quit university and get a job.
7. You're not going to learn how to use the new office computer.
8. You're going to tell the boss about one of your colleagues who is always late.
9. You're going to buy a house.
10. You're not going to take your vacation this year.
11. You're going to ask for an overseas transfer.
12. You're not going to save any money for your retirement years. Who knows what could happen before then?
13. You're going to walk out of the meeting if it gets too boring.
14. You're going to refuse a job transfer even though it means a promotion. You like living in this city.
15. Even though your union is going out on strike, you're going to keep on working.
16. You're going to hire your brother to be your assistant.
17. You're going to invest all your money in the stock market.
18. You're going to quit this class.
19. You're going to call in sick because you want just to stay home and relax for a day.
20. You're not going to attend the annual convention.
21. You're not going to practice the presentation you have to make to the Board of Directors next week because you don't have time.
22. You're not going to participate in any more class discussions.
23. You're going to retire when you're 50 years old.

24. You're going to take a year's leave of absence and travel around the world.
25. You're going to tell the boss you want a raise immediately or else you'll quit.

Exercise 3. Try to use a variety of phrases from the unit in discussing the following situations.

Student A: Give an opinion.

Student B: Try to persuade Student A to change his [or her] mind.

Student A: Counterargue.

Student B: Try again to persuade Student A.

Student A: Counterargue or concede.

1. A small local bookstore should [should not] spend all its advertising budget on television advertising.
2. The government should reduce [increase, abolish] taxes.
3. It's a good policy [a bad policy] for large companies to regularly transfer young executives from place to place to give them more experience.
4. Now is a good time [a bad time] to invest in gold.
5. Employees should [should not] complain to the manager if a supervisor gives them a poor performance evaluation.
6. The company should [should not] pay for every executive to have an annual medical check-up.
7. Job applicants should never tell [should explain to] the interviewer that they hate their present jobs.
8. It's all right [never all right] for an employee who feels overworked to take a day of sick leave to go to the beach.
9. Wage payments should [should not] be linked to productivity.
10. Video games should [should not] be banned.
11. A company has the right [does not have the right] to prohibit its workers from taking on second jobs.
12. It's okay [not okay] for a job applicant to lie about past job experience in order to get a better job.
13. The government should [should not] take responsibility for day care centers for children of working parents.
14. Female employees should [should not] be given longer maternity leave.
15. A company should [should not] pay for an executive to take a wife or husband on a business trip.

16. A company should sponsor more [fewer] social activities such as sports teams, picnics or trips.
17. The best [most inefficient] way to get the job done is to do it yourself.
18. A company should [should not] allow people married to each other to work in the same office.
19. Employees should feel free [should never try] to discuss personal problems with their managers.
20. It's impossible [possible] to judge whether a job applicant is suitable after only a one-hour interview.
21. It's acceptable [unacceptable] for workers to quit without giving two weeks' notice.
22. A woman should not [should feel free to] work outside the home if she has young children.
23. Most people work for the money [for job satisfaction].
24. Most workers like [hate] responsibility.
25. Factory workers should [should not] be allowed to exchange work assignments with others.
26. A manager should always be available [should be available by appointment only] for subordinates to talk to.
27. Doctors should [should not] be allowed to advertise prices of certain services.
28. The government should [should not] allow teachers to go out on strike.
29. Managers should [should not] try to deal with employees' personal problems.
30. Making decisions in a group is the best way to solve a problem [is a big waste of time].

Communication Concepts

Nonverbal Communication

Nonverbal communication involves sending messages without using words. Think, for example, how people can communicate the following feelings and ideas without saying a single word:

"Yes."   "I'd like to say something."
"No."   "This is boring."
"I don't know."   "Calm down."
"Wait a minute."   "I feel impatient."

These messages are communicated through the use of eye contact, facial expressions, gestures, and body posture.

Nonverbal communication can actually express more than verbal communication. However, these nonverbal messages are not always the same in different cultures. For instance, eye contact can be interpreted in various ways. In some cultures speakers are expected to look directly at the listeners, while in other cultures it is a sign of disrespect to look somebody directly in the eye. For speakers participating in meetings with English speakers, it is important to understand how they use these nonverbal messages. Here are some examples:

Eye contact

1. Speakers who look directly at group members seem more self-confident and sure of themselves. Thus, group members are more likely to be persuaded by a speaker who maintains eye contact with them.
2. When listeners look at the speaker, they show that they are listening. By showing that they are paying attention, listeners encourage speakers to express their ideas.
3. One way people can show they're willing to speak is to look directly at the group leader.
4. If speakers do not want to speak or participate in the discussion, they usually do not establish eye contact with the group leader.
5. Group members may be able to quiet someone who is talking too much by avoiding eye contact.
6. It is possible for the group leader to bring members into the discussion just by looking directly at them.

Facial expressions

7. Group members can encourage a speaker to continue by smiling or nodding their heads.
8. By frowning or raising an eyebrow, listeners can let the speaker know that they don't understand the message or that they disagree.

Body posture

9. By leaning forward, a person can show agreement or interest and thus encourage a speaker.
10. By leaning forward, a person can also show his [or her] intention to speak.
11. By leaning backward, a person can show disagreement or lack of interest and thus discourage the speaker.

12. A person with folded arms may look closed to the discussion. This can discourage interaction.

Gestures

13. Group members can request permission to speak by raising a hand or a finger. In informal groups, however, members do not usually raise their hands before speaking.
14. If someone is trying to interrupt, the speaker may put out his [or her] hand. This is a signal that the person should allow the speaker to finish talking.

What other messages can you think of that can be sent nonverbally? Can you think of some ways these messages change from culture to culture?

Discussion Techniques

Summarizing

At certain points in the discussion it is useful for the leader to summarize what has happened so far. This is often done to test for consensus—to see whether the members are ready to agree on a particular point. Also, a leader often summarizes what has been decided so far before going on to another point. Some phrases to use in summarizing a discussion are:

Let's summarize what we've $\left\{ \begin{array}{l} \text{decided} \\ \text{agreed on} \end{array} \right\}$ so far.

Do we agree that _____?

Then we agree that _____?

So far, we've $\left\{ \begin{array}{l} \text{decided} \\ \text{agreed} \end{array} \right\}$ that _____.

In addition, the leader usually summarizes final conclusions the group has reached at the end of the discussion:

In $\left\{ \begin{array}{l} \text{conclusion,} \\ \text{summary,} \end{array} \right\}$ _____.

To $\left\{ \begin{array}{l} \text{summarize,} \\ \text{conclude,} \end{array} \right\}$ _____.

Role Playing

Role Play 10A: A "Go-Between"

Situation

A Western-based multinational construction company does a great deal of business in developing nations. The sales director of this company has been contacted by a "go-between" in one of these countries. This go-between will guarantee the firm a major government contract if the company pays him $1 million. The sales director realizes that in this country such payments are a part of normal business practice. In fact, $1 million is not much compared to the huge profits of the deal. Without making such payments over the years, the company would have lost millions, perhaps billions, of dollars worth of business. The company has made payments before to this go-between and he has always delivered what he promised.

The problem now is that the company has a new managing director. This new director has recently made a public statement that the company will no longer make questionable payments to officials for "assisting" with contracts. The managing director regards these payments as bribes, not as normal operating expenses. Since the sales director believes that these payments are absolutely necessary if the company is going to continue to operate in these countries, he [or she] has asked for a meeting.

Purpose of the Discussion

The purpose of this discussion is for the group members to agree on a company policy regarding doing business with go-betweens.

Group Roles

Leader: the president of the company
The new managing director
The sales director(s)

Observing: Evaluating the Discussion

1. *Listening to the discussion*

As you listen to the discussion, make a list of the major points that the group members discuss.

_____

_____

_____

_____

_____

2. *Rating the discussion*

Use the following scales to rate the discussion:

a. *Overall performance*

4	3	2	1	0
excellent	good	average	weak	failing

b. *Participation*

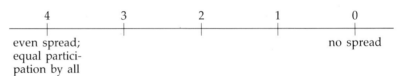

4	3	2	1	0
even spread; equal participation by all				no spread

c. *Interaction*

4	3	2	1	0
much interaction among members				no interaction among members

d. *Problem Solving*

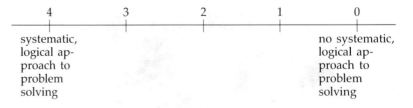

4	3	2	1	0
systematic, logical approach to problem solving				no systematic, logical approach to problem solving

e. *Leader control*

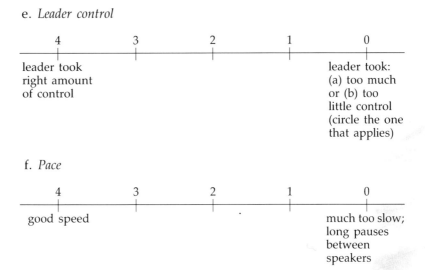

4	3	2	1	0

leader took
right amount
of control

leader took:
(a) too much
or (b) too
little control
(circle the one
that applies)

f. *Pace*

4	3	2	1	0

good speed

much too slow;
long pauses
between
speakers

Role Play 10B: Banning Nonprescription Drugs

Situation

The government of a country has just banned almost 2,000 nonpre-scription drugs from the market. These drugs include vitamins, cough syrups, stomach upset pills, and pain tablets. The government believes that these drugs are harmful, ineffective, or simply unneces-sary. Officials say that this ban will protect citizens from wasting their money on drugs they don't need. Drug company executives, on the other hand, say that these drugs certainly are not harmful. In fact, these drugs are much in demand. Citizens should have the right to buy whatever they want. Such a ban might open up a black market in substandard products. The government has asked a visiting United Nations official to study the situation. A meeting has been called to discuss the issue.

Purpose of the Discussion

The purpose of this discussion is for the group members to agree on the best government policy concerning the sale of nonprescription drugs.

Group Roles

Leader: the visiting United Nations official
Government representative(s)
Drug company representative(s)

Observing: Evaluating the Discussion

1. *Listening to the discussion*

As you listen to the discussion, make a list of the major points that the group members discuss.

_____

_____

_____

_____

_____

2. *Rating the discussion*

Use the following scales to rate the discussion:

a. *Overall performance*

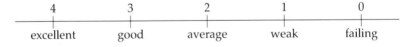

4	3	2	1	0
excellent	good	average	weak	failing

b. *Participation*

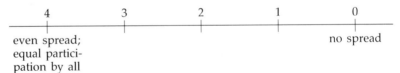

4   3   2   1   0

even spread;   no spread
equal partici-
pation by all

c. *Interaction*

4   3   2   1   0

much inter-   no interaction
action among   among mem-
members   bers

d. *Problem Solving*

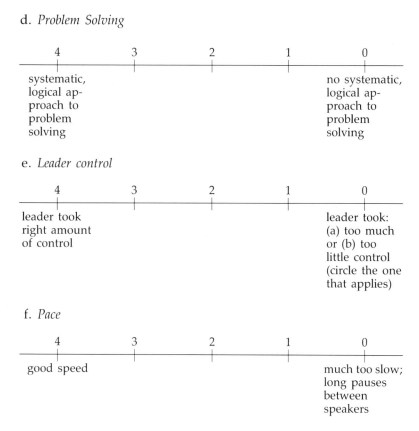

4	3	2	1	0

systematic, logical approach to problem solving

no systematic, logical approach to problem solving

e. *Leader control*

4	3	2	1	0

leader took right amount of control

leader took: (a) too much or (b) too little control (circle the one that applies)

f. *Pace*

4	3	2	1	0

good speed

much too slow; long pauses between speakers

Role Play 10C: A Problem of Pollution

Situation

A town of about 100,000 people is located in a valley. About 30 years ago industries such as oil refineries and fertilizer manufacturers began moving into the area. Now there are about 25 factories located here because of the good location and available raw materials. The problem, however, is that this area is one of the most polluted in the world. Because the wind cannot blow the pollution over the mountains, it remains in the valley. The hillsides are covered with dead plants and trees. Fish in the city's rivers are deformed and blind. The infant death rate is 35% and birth defects are frequent. About 25% of the factory workers have lung diseases and 35% of the workers' children have severe breathing problems.

Workers have demanded that something be done immediately to solve this dangerous situation. The problem is that the government budget has been hurt by the current recession. Government officials do not want to close down these industries since they are vital to the country's economy. Factory officials say that they have also been hurt by the recession. They cannot afford to install expensive pollution control devices. In addition, if the factories are forced to close, all of the workers will lose their jobs. With the recession, they will not be able to find other work. However, the present situation cannot be allowed to continue. Industry officials have suggested that workers move to a less polluted area. Workers, however, say that they cannot afford to move or to pay daily transportation to and from work. A government official has called a meeting to discuss the issue.

Purpose of the Discussion

The purpose of this discussion is for the group members to agree on the best way to solve the serious problem of pollution in this area.

Group Roles

Leader: a government official
Industry official(s)
Representative(s) of the factory workers

Observing: Evaluating the Discussion

1. *Listening to the discussion*

   As you listen to the discussion, make a list of the major points that the group members discuss.

   _____

   _____

   _____

   _____

   _____

2. *Rating the discussion*

Use the following scales to rate the discussion:

a. *Overall performance*

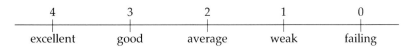

4	3	2	1	0
excellent	good	average	weak	failing

b. *Participation*

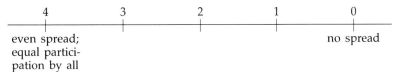

4	3	2	1	0
even spread; equal partici- pation by all				no spread

c. *Interaction*

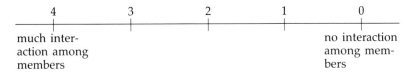

4	3	2	1	0
much inter- action among members				no interaction among mem- bers

d. *Problem Solving*

4	3	2	1	0
systematic, logical ap- proach to problem solving				no systematic, logical ap- proach to problem solving

e. *Leader control*

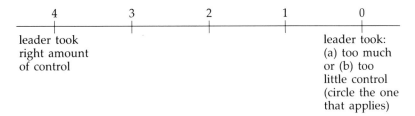

4	3	2	1	0
leader took right amount of control				leader took: (a) too much or (b) too little control (circle the one that applies)

f. *Pace*

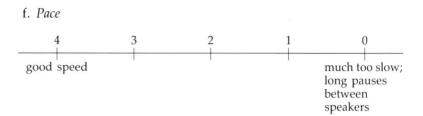

Role Play 10D: Dismissing Unproductive Employees

Situation

A joint-venture company (owned by an Asian company and a Western company) is operating a manufacturing subsidiary in the Asian country. Lately there have been some conflicts between Asian and Western executives over company policy. In traditional Asian companies staff promotions are based on length of service and level of education. Furthermore, large companies usually offer lifetime guaranteed employment. Western companies, however, usually base pay raises and promotions on merit. It is usual practice to dismiss inefficient or unproductive workers. Now that the company is faced with financial difficulties, it has become necessary to make major cutbacks in expenditures. However, Western and Asian executives disagree over where to make these cutbacks.

The current problem involves two Asian managers. Although all of the executives agree that these managers are incompetent, the executives disagree over how to handle the problem. Asian executives believe that it is not fair to dismiss these employees who have been with the company for almost 15 years. Western executives, on the other hand, feel that it is in the best interests of the company to get rid of unproductive workers. These executives believe that in order to survive, the company must decrease its work force.

The chairman of the Board of Directors has called a meeting to discuss this issue.

Purpose of the Discussion

The purpose of this discussion is for the group members to agree on a company policy regarding the dismissal of employees.

Group Roles

Leader: the chairman of the Board of Directors
Western executive(s)
Asian executive(s)

Observing: Evaluating the Discussion

1. *Listening to the discussion*

As you listen to the discussion, make a list of the major points that the group members discuss.

_____

_____

_____

_____

_____

2. *Rating the discussion*

Use the following scales to rate the discussion:

a. *Overall performance*

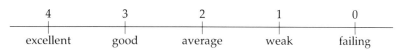

b. *Participation*

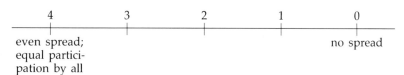

c. *Interaction*

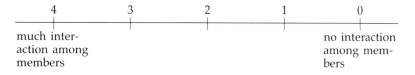

d. *Problem Solving*

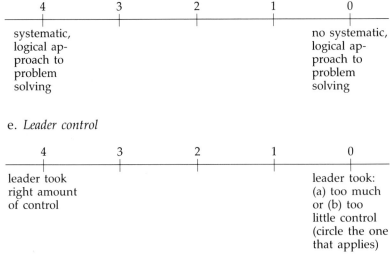

e. *Leader control*

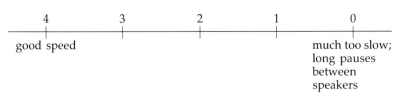

f. *Pace*

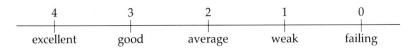

Final Participant Self-Evaluation

1. *Final evaluation*

After you participate in a discussion, use the following scales to rate your own performance:

a. *Accuracy:* How well did you express yourself? How well did you use correct grammar and vocabulary?

4	3	2	1	0
excellent	good	average	weak	failing

b. *Use of phrases:* Did you appropriately use a wide variety of phrases?

4	3	2	1	0
excellent	good	average	weak	failing

c. *Interaction:* Did you use many different functions?

4	3	2	1	0
excellent	good	average	weak	failing

d. *Involvement:* Did you speak about the right amount? Did you initiate? Did you involve others?

4	3	2	1	0
excellent	good	average	weak	failing

e. *Content:* Were all of your comments on the subject? Did you support your ideas?

4	3	2	1	0
excellent	good	average	weak	failing

2. *Improvement*

Answer the following questions:

a. How do you think you've improved your speaking skills since the beginning of the course?

_____

_____

b. Which activities do you think have helped you improve the most?

_____

_____

_____

_____

Useful Vocabulary

Listening Practice

Section 1 company headquarters

Section 2 sales rep
to automate

Controlled Practice

Exercise 2 to disconnect the phone
sales clerk
leave of absence

Exercise 3 to abolish
to link
video game
to ban
maternity leave
to sponsor
to exchange
to be available

Communication Concepts

eye contact
facial expression
gesture
body posture
culture
disrespect
self-confident
to maintain
to avoid
to frown
to lean

Role Playing

10A "go-between"
huge
to deliver
questionable payments
bribe
operating expenses

10B   in demand
            black market
            substandard products

10C   fertilizer
            raw materials
            polluted
            infant death rate
            birth defect
            vital
            to install
            pollution control device

10D   joint-venture company
            manufacturing subsidiary
            to get rid of
            to survive

Appendices

Appendix I: This form includes criteria for evaluating individual participants. A complete explanation of how to use this form can be found in the Instructor's Manual.

Appendix II: This form can be used for commenting on individual performances. Instructors may wish to use this form as a guide in designing their own form to fit standard-size paper. They can then photocopy as many forms as they need.

Appendix III: This evaluation form can be used to judge the overall performance of a discussion group.

Appendix IV: Students and/or instructors can develop their own role plays by following these guidelines.

Appendix I

Individual Evaluation Grading Criteria

excellent	good	average	weak	failing
4	3	2	1	0

Accuracy

4	3	2	1	0
precisely conveys message with few grammar/ lexical errors	clearly conveys message, with some noticeable grammar/lexical errors	manages to convey message despite frequent grammar/lexical errors	many grammar/ lexical errors at times interfere with message; *or* insufficient number of utterances to judge accuracy	serious grammar/ lexical errors block communications

Use of Phrases

4	3	2	1	0
effective and accurate use of a wide variety of phrases	appropriate and usually accurate use of different phrases	generally appropriate and accurate use of a limited number of phrases (not including "Excuse me" or "I think")	rote use of a few phrases; *or* inappropriate or inaccurate use of phrases	no use of phrases

Interaction

4	3	2	1	0
effectively and appropriately uses a wide variety of functions such as • clarifying • comparing • supporting • opposing • persuading • counterarguing	appropriately uses different functions such as • asking questions • suggesting • advising • getting further information	appropriately uses such functions as • giving opinions • making statements • agreeing • disagreeing	responds by answering questions	does not interact with others

202

Involvement

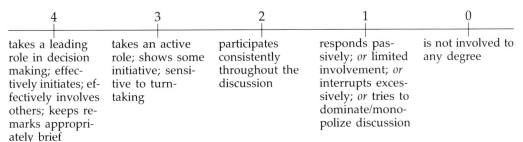

4	3	2	1	0
takes a leading role in decision making; effectively initiates; effectively involves others; keeps remarks appropriately brief	takes an active role; shows some initiative; sensitive to turn-taking	participates consistently throughout the discussion	responds passively; *or* limited involvement; *or* interrupts excessively; *or* tries to dominate/monopolize discussion	is not involved to any degree

Relevant Content

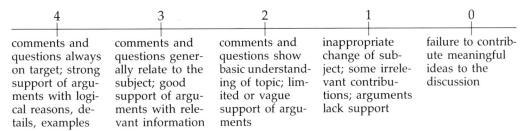

4	3	2	1	0
comments and questions always on target; strong support of arguments with logical reasons, details, examples	comments and questions generally relate to the subject; good support of arguments with relevant information	comments and questions show basic understanding of topic; limited or vague support of arguments	inappropriate change of subject; some irrelevant contributions; arguments lack support	failure to contribute meaningful ideas to the discussion

Leadership

(Use this scale for the group leader, in place of Relevant Content. Leadership tasks include giving a clear and appropriate introduction and closing; including quiet members; controlling members who try to talk too much; keeping the discussion on the subject; keeping the discussion moving; clarifying and summarizing when necessary; giving an opinion when needed.)

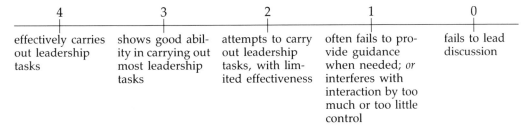

4	3	2	1	0
effectively carries out leadership tasks	shows good ability in carrying out most leadership tasks	attempts to carry out leadership tasks, with limited effectiveness	often fails to provide guidance when needed; *or* interferes with interaction by too much or too little control	fails to lead discussion

Appendix II

Individual Evaluation Form

Name			
Role			
Total Points			
Accuracy			
Use of Phrases			
Interaction			
Involvement			
Relevant Content			

Time:
  Begin:
  End:

Name			
Role			
Total Points			
Accuracy			
Use of Phrases			
Interaction			
Involvement			
Relevant Content			

Time:
  Begin:
  End:

Appendix III

General Group Evaluation

Evaluator: _____ Topic: _____

Participants: _____

Overall Performance

4	3	2	1	0
excellent	good	average	weak	very poor

Participation

4	3	2	1	0
even spread; equal partici- pation by all				little spread

Clarity

4	3	2	1	0
listeners able to understand everything				listeners able to understand nothing

Interaction

4	3	2	1	0
much interac- tion among members				no interaction among mem- bers

Problem Solving

4	3	2	1	0
systematic, logical ap- proach to problem solving				no systematic, logical ap- proach to problem solving

Leader Control

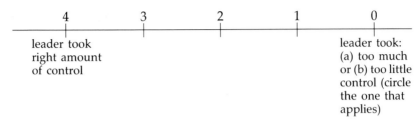

```
      4          3          2          1          0
──────┼──────────┼──────────┼──────────┼──────────┼──────
   leader took                            leader took:
   right amount                           (a) too much
   of control                             or (b) too little
                                          control (circle
                                          the one that
                                          applies)
```

Pace

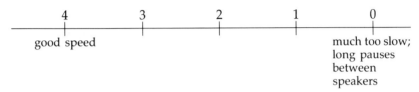

```
      4          3          2          1          0
──────┼──────────┼──────────┼──────────┼──────────┼──────
   good speed                             much too slow;
                                          long pauses
                                          between
                                          speakers
```

Topic

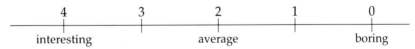

```
      4          3          2          1          0
──────┼──────────┼──────────┼──────────┼──────────┼──────
   interesting            average              boring
```

Appendix IV

Developing Your Own Role Plays

In order to provide a variety of interesting and relevant discussion topics, you can develop your own role plays. These role plays may be written by the students—individually, in pairs, or in small groups. Of course, they may also be written by the teacher. Here are instructions to the students for developing role plays.

1. Choose a problem in class, at work, in the community, or in the country where you live. You can often find good ideas in newspapers or magazines.
2. Write a brief explanation of the problem in one paragraph. Be sure that the conflict is clearly stated.
3. Decide on the different roles that should be represented in the discussion.
4. Write out the role play following the plan of the role plays in this book: (1) situation; (2) purpose of the discussion; and (3) group roles.
5. Put a title on your role play.
6. Hand in this role play to the instructor, including your name(s) on the paper.
7. Work with the instructor to make any necessary changes in the role play.
8. The instructor will assign the role play to your group or perhaps to another group. Pay attention as the role play is performed in class. Decide whether any changes should be made. Can you improve the explanation of the situation? Is more information needed, or is there some information that could be left out? Is the purpose of the discussion clear? Should any of the roles be changed?
9. Hand in a final copy of the role play to the instructor.